RELIGIONS
OF
AFRICA

Volumes in the Religious Traditions of the World Series

Edited by H. Byron Earhart

RELIGIONS
OF
AFRICA

Traditions in Transformation

E. THOMAS LAWSON

1817

HARPER & ROW, PUBLISHERS, SAN FRANCISCO
Cambridge, Hagerstown, New York, Philadelphia
London, Mexico City, São Paulo, Singapore, Sydney

On the cover: "Horned Goddess," a rock shelter painting dated at 1500 BCE, discovered in 1956 at Tassili Aouarhet in the Hoggar Mountains of the Central Sahara Desert.

RELIGIONS OF AFRICA: *Traditions in Transformation.*
Copyright © 1985 by E. Thomas Lawson. All rights reserved.
Printed in the United States of America. No part of this book may
be used or reproduced in any manner whatsoever without written
permission except in the case of brief quotations embodied in
critical articles and reviews. For information address Harper &
Row, Publishers, Inc., 10 East 53rd Street, New York, NY
10022. Published simultaneously in Canada by Fitzhenry &
Whiteside, Limited, Toronto.

FIRST EDITION

Designed by Donna Davis

Library of Congress Cataloging in Publication Data

Lawson, E. Thomas.
  Religions of Africa

  (Religious traditions of the world)

  Bibliography: p.
  Includes index.
  1. Zulus—Religion. 2. Yorubas—Religion. I. Title. II. Series.
BL2480.Z8L39   1984   299'.683   84–47729
ISBN 0-06-065211-X

89 90   10 9 8 7 6 5 4

for Ruth, Sonya, and Jennifer

Contents

EDITOR'S FOREWORD

Religious Traditions of the World

O ne of human history's most fascinating aspects is the richness and variety of its religious traditions—from the earliest times to the present, in every area of the world. The ideal way to learn about all these religions would be to visit the homeland of each—to discuss the scriptures or myths with members of these traditions, explore their shrines and sacred places, view their customs and rituals. Few people have the luxury of leisure and money to take such trips, of course; nor are many prepared to make a systematic study of even those religions that are close at hand. Thus this series of books is a substitute for an around-the-world trip to many different religious traditions: it is an armchair pilgrimage through a number of traditions both distant and different from one another, as well as some situated close to one another in time, space, and religious commitment.

Individual volumes in this series focus on one or more religions, emphasizing the distinctiveness of each tradition while considering it within a comparative context. What links the volumes as a series is a shared concern for religious traditions and a common format for discussing them. Generally, each volume will explore the history of a tradition, interpret it as a unified set of religious beliefs and practices, and give examples of religious careers and typical practices. Individual volumes are self-contained treatments and can be taken up in any sequence. They are introductory, providing interested readers with an overall interpretation of religious traditions without presupposing prior knowledge.

The author of each book combines special knowledge of a religious tradition with considerable experience in teaching and communicating an interpretation of that tradition. This special knowledge includes familiarity with various languages, investigation of religious texts and historical development, and direct contact with the peoples and practices under study. The authors have refined their special knowledge through many years of teaching and writing to frame a general interpretation of the tradition that is responsible to the best-known facts and is readily available to the interested reader.

Let me join with the authors of the series in wishing you an enjoyable and profitable experience in learning about religious traditions of the world.

H. Byron Earhart
Series Editor

Preface

A preface is the appropriate place to declare intentions and acknowledge indebtedness. Though this book is entitled *Religions of Africa*, it lays no claim to being comprehensive; a comprehensive treatment of the religions of Africa would be impossible within the covers of one book. Depending upon how one defines religious traditions, there are either hundreds or thousands of religions in Africa. The aims of this work are more modest. It is my intention to introduce the student to some of the religions of Africa by describing the world view they embody and the acts that illustrate it. I also intend to show that these are living and lively traditions in process of transformation, possessing profound internal resources to respond to new situations and modes of thought with creativity and depth.

My indebtedness runs deep. For the Zulu material, three works provided the informative bedrock on which my superstructure was built. These are Eileen Jensen Krige's classic *The Social System of the Zulus*, Axel-Ivar Berglund's illuminating *Zulu Thought-Patterns and Symbolism*, and Bengt G. M. Sundkler's *Bantu Prophets in South Africa*. Each of these three volumes is a treasure house of information and detailed description of ritual practices and beliefs. I recommend them to all students who wish to move beyond this introductory text.

After reading through many books on the Yoruba, I decided that three of them provided particularly significant information about the Yoruba religious system. These are J. Omosade Awolalu's *Yoruba Beliefs and Sacrificial Rites*, E. Bolaji Idowu's *Olodumare: God in Yoruba Belief*, and J. D. Y. Peel's *Aladura: A Religious Movement Among the Yoruba*. Each is an outstanding work and provides the kind of precise detail necessary for general summaries. But all the books listed in the bibliography were helpful in the formative stages of this work.

I am also indebted to the Yoruba people who so willingly acted as informants to me. I am particularly grateful to Emmanuel Oladepo Alaye, who, over a three-month period, spent many hours a

1

week giving me firsthand information about his traditions. He was at all times patient and gracious.

I am thankful to Western Michigan University for making access to the Dec-10 computer so easy and painless. Working on a terminal rather than at a typewriter speeded the process of writing considerably and made the correction of mistakes bearable.

And I am indebted to my wife, Ruth, and my two daughters, Sonya and Jennifer, for reading and criticizing the manuscript in its various stages and for providing spiritual support when I thought the marathon would never end. This book is dedicated to them.

Finally, I am indebted to my many students, who have sat through my course on African Religions over the years and taught me what would work and what would not.

E. T. L.

■

CHAPTER I

Introduction

Perceptions of Africa

The Africa known by tourists is a vast continent punctuated with modern, skyscrapered cities that are encroaching on game reserves populated by freely roaming wild animals, little villages with thatched roofs on circular huts, grass plains merging into dense and often impenetrable jungles, and black people clothed in colorful garments or nothing at all. For those not given to travel but to reading novels, watching television, going to the movies, and reading the local newspaper, it is both the land of three-million-year-old Lucy, whose fossilized bones testify to the origins of the ancestors of homo sapiens, and the land of Tarzan and the apes. And for some it is the dark continent of bizarre ritual practices and farfetched stories about the origins of the world and the beings who inhabit it.

This is a book about some of the religious traditions of Africa. In it we shall consider these seemingly bizarre practices and ideas. Our purpose is to place them in a context in which they may be more readily understood. In this attempt at understanding the modes of thought and practice of people who, at least on the surface, lead lives quite different from ours in the West, we follow the paths of an illustrious band of inquirers who have preceded us. Inquiry into the traditions of Africa has been going on for a long time, and over the last few decades there has been an increasing interest, both scholarly and popular, in the worlds of Africa.

But despite a developing interest in Africa spurred by the establishment of the Peace Corps in the sixties, the recent paleontological discoveries, and various revolutions and coups, Africa still carries the image of the dark continent, a vast geographical area that is little known, essentially backward, and rather mysterious. This is surprising, because Africa has been explored and studied for a long time. The Phoenicians had already circumnavigated the continent in the sixth century B.C. Vasco da Gama and Bartholomew Dias explored it as a route to India four hundred years ago, and the Dutch had begun to settle its southern regions by the mid-seventeenth century.

Serious scientific study of this land is more recent but is at least a hundred years old; it is not as if Africa is a newly discovered Atlantis. Yet Africa does need to be rediscovered, because its story is our own. We are all Africans. For it is in Africa that the human race began—a few million years ago. This story of our origins as a species is still being written; anthropologists and other scientists continue to search for further clues to fill in the outlines of the story.

It is in Africa, too, that the first cultural discoveries were made, discoveries we now take for granted. For example, it was in Africa that the first tool was invented, the first fire lit by a human hand, the first crop planted, the first village established, the first language spoken. These activities are some of the marks of human civilization. The original humans then began their slow journey to other continents, where they began to establish a wide range of life-styles. This story of our African origins has been painstakingly assembled during the last century; it is now a basic assumption of Western scientific thought. To this day, of course, many African peoples continue to retell their own stories of beginnings. The content of their stories is different from the story we have been writing recently, but the interest in origins is identical to our own and testifies to the same seriousness of intellectual purpose.

The Reality of Africa

What is the context for the religious traditions we shall be examining? How can the dark continent become illumined for us? We shall start by learning something about the realities of Africa.

Africa is the second largest of the continents on our planet. Its actual population today is estimated to be about four hundred million. The land consists of thick forests, high plateaus covered with tall grasses and acacia trees, and severe deserts. An astonishing variety of human societies occupy its land areas, and a wide range of languages reverberate on its streets and pathways. In the Niger-Congo language family alone there are nine hundred languages, each having numerous dialects; the **Bantu*** languages, each consisting of many forms, are only one subgroup of this vast array of languages in the Niger-Congo family.

The sheer massiveness of Africa is sufficient to overwhelm anyone who wishes to study some aspect of its contours, whether interested in languages, human origins, social organization, political change, or animal life. Decisions have to be made, therefore, as to what one will study. Some generally accepted divisions have been accepted by most scholars; for example, the continent is usually divided into two parts for investigation.

One area of study starts at the Mediterranean and reaches to the lower edge of the Sahara Desert. This is usually known as Islamic Africa. The other area of study consists of the rest of the continent and is known as sub-Saharan Africa, or black Africa. Such a term is quite misleading, for the people of Africa below the Sahara come in many shades, sizes, and traditions. And despite the fact that the upper part of Africa is known as Islamic Africa, it is not true that Islam has had no influence below the Sahara. In fact, over the centuries Islam has vigorously pursued a policy of conversion and has been quite successful in many sub-Saharan countries. It has made great strides in Nigeria in the last few centuries, and the **Yoruba**, one of the peoples we shall be studying, have been partially converted to it.

We shall focus upon the religious life of people in the sub-Saharan part of Africa. Many books have been written about these Africans. There are also many books about "primitive religions" in which these peoples and their religious traditions are lumped together with small-scale societies from Polynesia, South America, North America, and even the Arctic. The assumption in these books is that such widely disparate societies have something important in common. But there is little agreement as to precisely what that is; often it means little more than that such people have not used writing as a form of cultural expression and that they are "small-scale." We shall not use the term *primitive* in this book; nor shall we operate according to any of its assumptions. We shall avoid lumping together all the people of sub-Saharan Africa, and we shall not ar-

---

*Terms defined in the Glossary are printed in boldface where they first appear in the text.

gue that they are all alike. Nothing could be further from the truth.

One of the realities of Africa is its diversity. This can be seen in the fact that its societies exhibit a wide range of social organization. Some are vast kingdoms with millions of subjects, thus belying the term *small-scale*. Nigeria is a good example of such a society. Others are small groups of families wandering in the hot sands of the Kalahari Desert. Some Africans from the earliest times developed town life, for example, the Yoruba of West Africa. Other Africans, such as the Zulu of South Africa, have lived for centuries in small villages.

Political arrangements also vary considerably from society to society. Some political systems are centrally controlled under the absolute rule of a king. Others are almost completely decentralized, with power in the hands of a village council or a village headman. Still others have a tribal organization, with authority residing in a chief. And others consist of small wandering bands dependent for a living on hunting and gathering and governed by consensus.

Of course, the coming of the Europeans and the Muslims changed some of these social and political arrangements. New boundaries were carved out of the old territories, resulting in the division of cultural wholes. New styles of politics were introduced. In Nigeria the British used the principle of indirect rule to control the population and gave to the chiefs powers they had never had before. Some of the problems encountered in Africa today are the direct result of the artificial boundaries and political structures imposed by the colonial powers.

The coming of the Muslims and Europeans also introduced new religious ideas and practices. Islam and Christianity in their various forms were carried to most of the African societies. What is clear is that neither Islam nor Christianity was successful in eradicating the traditional religious thought and practices of the societies into which they were introduced. Though Muslim and Christian symbols are everywhere in evidence in Africa, they are often merely an additional element in the religious life of the people. We shall have occasion later to pay some attention to the relationship between the indigenous religions and the introduced religions. In this introduction we need only say that over the last century, especially, there have been religiously based movements that have arisen to resist these external religious traditions. These new religious movements, identical with neither Christianity nor Islam nor, for that matter, the indigenous religions, have been powerful forces, expressing not only political and nationalistic power but a new kind of religious creativity. Some scholars have gone so far as to argue that an understanding and explanation of the causes and functions of these new religions will provide important clues to the nature of religion wherever it is found.

Some of these new religious movements have appropriated symbols from traditional African religions but given them a new twist. Other movements have employed Christian imagery and given it a novel interpretation. Some have developed followings with thousands of members; others, after a brief moment of glory, have withered away as their leaders have died or been killed.

Not only have these new religious movements been examples of religious creativity, they have also been vehicles for the expression of the demand for independence, equality, freedom, and nationhood. Those governments interested in "keeping the natives in their place" have shown considerable interest in these movements and expressed fear of them because of their involvement in the forces for social change.

For those scholars who wish to make a clear distinction between religious and political action, these movements have proved to be particularly difficult to analyze. This should not be at all surprising when one considers that a people with a long tradition of their own have developed an elaborate world view. If change does occur, it will be within the terms of that world view. Whatever is novel in any society is at least partly traceable to one or more elements in the world view that has developed over time. Two countries, Nigeria and South Africa, have proven to be especially fertile areas for the development of new religions.

Many scholars have remarked upon the proliferation of new religious movements in the Republic of South Africa, a nation with four million whites who effectively control the lives of twenty-five million Africans. Though many of these religious movements employ Christian imagery, such imagery is often combined with strong anti-white sentiment. Some scholars, therefore, tend to downplay the religious dimensions of these movements and interpret them as political movements in religious garb. But the situation is far more complex. In the case of the Zulu we see a complex symbol system in place that is quite capable of being transformed to deal with new situations in a new setting. Much the same is the case with such movements among the Yoruba of Nigeria. In the case of the Yoruba there is a complex and differentiated symbol system that not only has consistently undergone internal transformation but, when confronted with other radically alien systems, has been able to adapt and adjust certain elements within the system into new forms.

Whether one is examining the traditional religious systems or the innovations brought about by new religious movements, one still needs to develop an approach that will increase our understanding of the structure and dynamics of African religions. In deciding upon an approach we will first describe the paths we will not take.

It would be easy and tempting to develop a collection of over-arching generalizations about the religious life of Africans. With some imagination, it might be possible to identify certain themes in African beliefs and practices. Some books do just that, and they make interesting reading. Or we might attempt a personal odyssey. Starting in the south and journeying slowly to the Congo, we might describe briefly our encounters with the beliefs and practices of the people we meet. Or we might start out with a specific notion, such as the idea of "belief." Having defined what a belief is, we could then systematize the various beliefs of various African societies into a kind of catalogue of beliefs, and we might show that in some way everything that Africans believe we also believe in some way or another. Or we might decide to stay put and examine only one African society, delineating its thoughts and practices in a careful and systematic manner. Some of the most helpful books on Africa are those that do exactly that. Or we might simply attempt to be comprehensive on the basis of what is available.

We shall do none of these. We have already called attention to the vastness of Africa, its cultural and linguistic variety. Rather than spreading ourselves too thin, we shall narrow our focus down to two African peoples, the Zulu and the Yoruba. It is our hope that by such a narrowing of focus we shall be able to give a better and more comprehensible picture of what two particular African religious worlds look like.

In our discussion of these two religious traditions we shall try to show what their religious worlds are like and how they live and act within these frameworks. In describing their religious worlds we shall show that each consists, first, of special places that provide a ritual environment for the performing of religious acts. These special places provide the dramatic setting for religious activity. Secondly, such worlds consist of special roles that define the purpose of the actors in the religious drama. Thirdly, they consist of special powers, presences, or beings with which the actors form prescribed relationships within the dramatic setting. Once we have achieved familiarity with the religious places, roles, and powers, we shall be prepared for a description and analysis of religious activities. In other words, we will know something about how the Zulu and Yoruba live and act in a religious world.

In order to make these religious activities as informative as possible, we shall describe the many religious symbols that are present in, and inform, the actions that characterize the stages on life's way. We shall see how, at important periods of Zulu and Yoruba life, the religious world is a significant presence. The focus here will be on what Zulu and Yoruba traditions are and the way in which such ancient tranditions are still reflected in present forms of life and thought—even under conditions of change.

No religious world remains the same over long periods of time for reasons having to do both with the internal experience of the Zulu and Yoruba people and with the relationships between other religions, other people, other social and cultural forms. Among both the Zulu and the Yoruba other systems of thought and action have been introduced. As a creative response, old forms have been redefined and new forms have been developed. Old places, roles, and powers have attained new meanings, and new places, roles, and powers have been recognized. In other words, transformation of the tradition has taken place. We shall attempt to describe the interesting and complex relationships that these new forms have to the traditional ones and show how flexible a tradition can be.

The Zulu and the Yoruba, then, will provide the focus of our attention, and the notions of "religious system" and "religious action" will provide the lenses through which we can view their religion. We shall certainly discover that ideas such as "primitive" and "simple" do little to advance our understanding of other peoples and their religious thought and action.

The Zulu live in the southern part of the African continent. The Yoruba live in the western part of central Africa. These two peoples are widely separated and have different histories, different social and

political organizations, and different cultures and languages. They
are distinct enough in style and tradition to provide us with the basis
for individual analysis, as well as comparison. And yet they are not
completely unrelated. First, they do occupy the same continent. Second, many of the people now occupying the southeastern part of the
continent migrated from central Africa over the last two thousand
years, and so at least some continuity, however tenuous, can be assumed. The Zulu and the Yoruba have been the subject of both
scholarly and popular interest. In the case of the Zulu the popular
imagination associates them with the picture of the warrior coura-
geously fighting the British and the **Boers** (the white settlers of
Dutch extraction who colonized southern Africa in the seventeenth
century).

In the case of the Yoruba we have a complex image of **witchcraft**, **divination**, and art. In fact a recent novel on the practice of
witchcraft in New York City traces it back to the Yoruba. Although
widely separated from each other on the African continent and radically different from each other in social and religious institutions, the
Zulu and the Yoruba belong to the same language family, the Niger-Congo. Although consisting of hundreds of languages and dialects, this language family can be divided into six groups: the West
Atlantic, the Mande, the Voltaic, the Adamawa-Eastern, the Kwa,
and the Benue-Congo. Yoruba belongs to the Kwa group and Zulu
to the Benue-Congo. More than seven million people speak Yoruba,
and about four million speak Zulu.

Zulu belongs to a subgroup within the Benue-Congo called the
Bantu set of languages. They are called Bantu because the word for
"people" is *bantu* in this assortment of languages. So, for example,
when the Zulu give their account of the origins of Unkulunkulu,
the first human being, they use the word *bantu* to describe him and
the people who issue forth from him.

The Zulu and the Yoruba are happy choices for a number of
reasons. They both have been the subject of sufficient scholarly
study so that a good basis for analysis exists. They both have the
kind of systems that appear in similar forms in some other African
societies, so that a knowledge of their religions opens a door to
knowledge of other African religions. Understanding the religion of
the Zulu, for example, opens the door to understanding the religion
of the Swazi, Xhosa, and other Nguni people. Both Zulu and Yoru-

ba have also been subject to the forces of colonialism and Christianization, and new religious movements have appeared in both contexts. They also have systems sufficiently different so that comparison and contrast becomes interesting and fruitful.

Today the Zulu are still under the domination of the white South African government. The Yoruba are free and are an important part of the complex, modern state of Nigeria. But bound or free their religious systems continue to exist and to provide the basis for continuing traditional practices and inventing new ones. These flexible religious traditions are our subject.

Our focus on these religions of Africa will consist of showing how in each case their religious places, roles, powers, and actions are expressions of a coherent system of thought that informs the conduct of the lives of the people who participate in them. We shall not ignore the obvious diversity of practice and belief in each religion. Instead we shall lay the groundwork for showing that, even granting religious diversity, there is an underlying unity of thought that provides a set of profound answers to fundamental questions about what is real, important, personal, dangerous, and desirable.

Specifically, Chapter II will provide the setting for understanding Zulu religion, Chapter III for understanding Yoruba religion. Chapter IV will be an analysis of how individual participants in these religious traditions, the roles they occupy, and the actions they perform lead us to the conclusion that each religion is an example of a system of thought about the world and the place of human life in it.

■

CHAPTER II

The Zulu and Their Religious Tradition

The Origins of the Zulu People

The origins of the Zulu people are shrouded in the mists of oral tradition. But by using a variety of specialized methods, scholars have been able to penetrate the mists and discover some of the Zulu past. They have concluded that within the last two thousand years there have been a series of migrations of large numbers of people from central Africa into the southern part of the continent. These migrants from the "north" had a linguistic identity, and they are referred to as "Bantu-speaking peoples." This means that although these people spoke many different languages the languages were similar enough in form and structure to deserve a common name, "Bantu." Scholars chose the name Bantu because this word for "people" occurs in a large array of languages spoken by the migrants. These people slowly settled the southeastern area of Africa all the way down to what is now known as the province of Natal in the Republic of South Africa. As their occupation solidified, they began to form special groups. One large group is now known as the Nguni people. The Nguni group consisted of many tribes and clans: the Xhosa, the Fingo, the Tembu, the Pondo, the Swazi, and the Zulu. This process of migration and solidification into special groups, each with a distinct language, was complete by the seventeenth century.

The Zulu at this stage of development were one group of people among many. According to their own traditions, an ancestor named Malandela had two sons named Qwabe and Zulu. These two sons

Zululand in its African context.

became the chiefs of two clans. Chief Zulu extended his quest for territory until he came to the Mfolosi Valley, an area north of the Thukela River in the present-day province of Natal. There Chief Zulu settled. His clan remained stable and unremarkable until the renowned Zulu chief **Shaka** emerged as a dynamic leader and warrior. Shaka in a very short time welded many different clans together into one powerful kingdom. He was successful in this endeavor because he developed completely new methods of military conquest, establishing highly disciplined regiments of young men and inventing new ways of deploying them in battle. It is Shaka's prowess as a general that has captivated the imagination of Western novelists and filmmakers. Movies about the Zulu warrior continue to be made to this day.

Today there are about four million Zulu in South Africa. They

continue to live on a small portion of their original land in the
northeast section of Natal. However, many Zulu can be found
throughout South Africa working in the mines, as domestic ser-
vants, and in those positions in the world of industry and business
not reserved for whites. Even under such very difficult conditions
some Zulu have been able to attain a high level of education and
thus will be found either at the segregated universities provided by
the South African government or, in special cases, at one of the Eng-
lish-speaking universities, such as the University of Cape Town or
Rhodes University.

Recently, the government of South Africa declared a portion of
the province of Natal as the Zulu "homeland," which they named
Kwazulu. Supposedly, within this area the Zulu will finally have
some political rights. Whether or not this is the case, because this
greatly diminished area is not self-sufficient, the Zulu will be
forced to continue their dependence on white South Africa, with
its system of **apartheid**. Apartheid is a governmental policy intended to keep the various groups of people living in South Africa
separate from each other. Its practical effect is to keep all black
people in a position of servitude and without political rights of any
kind. The "homeland" is certainly far less in area than the traditional Zulu kingdom. At this moment the Zulu are strongly insist-
ing on their autonomy and freedom, and Zulu leaders have often
been some of the most eloquent spokesmen for the rights of all
black people in South Africa. In fact, the Zulu chief **Albert
Luthuli** was granted the Nobel Peace Prize for his articulate and
peaceful presentation of the case for all the oppressed people of
South Africa. And the present Zulu Chief, Gatsha Buthelezi, has
also acquired a reputation as a spokesman for the rights of Zulu
and other black people in South Africa.

While the Zulu people remain in such an oppressed situation it
is impossible to speak of an independent kingdom or nation, despite the recently proclaimed Kwazulu. But long before such a
proclamation, the buffeting that these people had received from
both British and Boer had already destroyed their autonomy.

In 1879 the British invaded the Zulu kingdom established by
Shaka and maintained by the succeeding chiefs. Cetshwayo was the
last of the Zulu kings or great chiefs. After the British invasion of
Zululand he was exiled; the invasion and his exile signaled the end

of Zulu territorial and political independence. In 1897 Zululand was ceded to the British colony of Natal. Shortly after this cession, the British and the **Afrikaaners** engaged in a war disastrous for both. This war created a deep enmity between the two white groups. In 1910 the Union of South Africa was formed as a state within the British Commonwealth. In 1913 the South African government promulgated the Native Land Act, naming a portion of traditional Zululand as a "native reserve." In fact, by 1906 much of the territory that the Zulu regarded as their own kingdom had already been overrun and was possessed by white Natal settlers of both British and Boer stock. It is the remnants of this native reserve that has now been designated as Kwazulu, the "homeland" of the Zulu people.

Despite this tragic ending to an illustrious history, Zulu social and religious traditions have survived. The Zulu have not forgotten their past, and even those Zulu who have become "Westernized" are very careful to insist upon the worth and significance of their own traditions. Of course, this does not mean that the Zulu are static. There have been changes, often subtle ones, in the Zulu world view. But there is clearly a continuity of thought and practice between present and past forms of Zulu life. In the town of Ulundi to this day on special occasions Chief Gatsha Buthelezi, dressed in traditional garb and carrying **assegai** and shield, assembles the men of the community into their regiments, and they sing the praises of their great ancestors, especially Shaka, who made of them one people.

The Religious System of the Zulu People

Though I have briefly called attention to the history of the Zulu, I do not intend to discuss the historical development of Zulu religion. There are many good reasons for not engaging in a historical analysis, the most important being lack of information. To study the historical development of a religious tradition means tracing its progress from its inception through its various changes to its present situation. Unfortunately, as with most African religions, such historical documentation is simply not available. We are dealing with an oral culture in which traditions are handed down by word of mouth. Documentation is not, of course, entirely

Kraals on the hills of Zululand. Photograph by the author.

lacking. We do have the diaries of Westerners who lived with the Zulu for a period. Some missionaries did make a very serious attempt to record the thought and practice of the Zulu. But such records are too sparse and too unsystematic to give us the kind of information that would permit significant historical analysis.

Rather than getting lost in unclear historical detail, I prefer to look directly at the known patterns of Zulu thought and practice. This way of studying a religion provides a key for opening the doors to at least some of the complex religious world of the Zulu. This approach starts out by viewing Zulu thought and practice as all of a piece. It assumes unity in Zulu life; through the changes brought about in history there is a continuity. Though such an approach acknowledges change, it insists that the Zulu religious system is flexible enough to deal with new situations in terms of its own ideas and practices.

A responsible description of the Zulu religious world must, however, choose some time frame, because, although history is not the focus, it cannot be ignored. It would be whistling in the dark to assert—without evidence—that the Zulu religious world of today is identical with that of five hundred years ago. In the first place, strictly speaking, Zulu identity can only be traced back as far as Chief Zulu, and some argue that it can only be traced back as far as Shaka. I have chosen to describe a system that has been in place for the last hundred and fifty years. Whatever documents we do have are from this period, and they are of sufficiently high quality to give us the kind of information we need. These documents are diaries, reports written by missionaries on the basis of interviews with Zulu, accounts by colonial administrators, and descriptions by various anthropologists and other social scientists. Obviously such documents reflect the biases of those who wrote them, and the information generated depends upon the kinds of questions asked. But they are sufficiently informative to provide us with the materials we need to provide a description of Zulu thought and practice.

Such thought and practice can be understood more clearly when we begin to identify their context. The Zulu people live and act in a religious world. This means that, whether one is talking about the birth of a child, a boy coming of age, the marriage of a young couple, or the death of a person in the family, there will be special places, people, and powers that give them special significance.

One way of getting a clearer view of the Zulu religious world is to pay attention to the places where religious acts take place, the roles assumed by the Zulu in the performance of these acts, the focus of the acts, and the style of action. In what follows, therefore, we shall organize our description of the Zulu religious system according to religious places, religious roles, religious powers, and religious acts.

As one wanders the dusty, red roads of present-day Zululand, one is struck by the simple beauty of the gently contoured green hills stretching to the horizon. These hills have great religious significance for the Zulu, for many of them provide the sites for the *kraal* or Zulu village. Some of these hills will not have kraals built on them, and it is such unpopulated hills that provide sites for special rituals the Zulu occasionally perform. But the Zulu kraal is the primary locus for ritual action. It is in this religious space that crucial religious performances occur periodically.

The kraal is the traditional village. It consists of a circular arrangement of thatched huts, each shaped something like a beehive. This circle of huts surrounds a circular cattle enclosure at the very center of the village. This inner circle is also called a kraal. So, in effect, you have a kraal within a kraal, a cattle enclosure within a

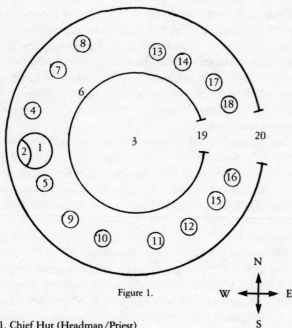

Figure 1.

1. Chief Hut (Headman/Priest)
2. Umsamo
3. Cattle Kraal
4, 5. Huts of Great Wife
6. Fence Enclosing Cattle Kraal
7, 8. Huts of Chief Wife of
       the Left Section
9, 10. Huts of Chief Wife
        of the Right Section
11, 12. Huts of the Sons
13, 14. Huts of the Daughters
15, 16, 17, 18. Huts for
                Guests and Visitors
19. Entrance to Cattle
    Kraal
20. Entrance to Village

human enclosure. The village is built on the side of the hill and slopes downward, with the entryways to both the outer circle of huts and the inner circle for the cattle facing toward the bottom of the hill. These entryways invariably face east.

The location of the huts in the circular arrangement is significant, for it indicates both social and ritual relationships of the occupants. The chief hut, on the west side of the circular arrangement, is the hut of the headman, who is also the priest of the kraal. This chief hut is balanced on each side by the huts of the headman's wives, one of whom will be known as the "great wife." Lower down are the huts for the children of the family, for appropriate relatives, and for guests or visitors. Such relatives, guests, or visitors will always have a particular association with this kraal, usually a relationship of kinship.

The inner circle is the cattle kraal. As with all Bantu-speaking peoples, cattle are of extreme practical and religious importance. It is in the cattle kraal that most of the important Zulu religious rituals are performed. In fact some scholars call the cattle enclosure the "temple" of the Zulu people. Although the particular inhabitants of a kraal might very well own other types of animals, such as sheep and goats, in the traditional Zulu village such other animals will be kept in separate enclosures outside the village proper. Only in cases of extreme poverty—a family that owns no cattle at all—will one find sheep or goats in the inner circle. Such a situation is much more likely today than it was in the heyday of the Zulu kingdom.

In each hut in the village will be found the **umsamo**. This is a special place set aside for various objects with ritual significance. In the hut of the headman/priest there will be found a very special umsamo. Its particular purpose is to provide a ritual ground for communing with the everpresent family ancestors. Likewise, on the west side of the inner cattle enclosure there is a ritual ground for the performance of religious ceremonies directed to the ancestors.

Besides the unoccupied but specially marked hills, then, the kraal turns out to be not only a place to live but a place to serve the ancestral powers in the manner that they require. Both places serve as sacred ground for the religious acts that the Zulu regularly perform.

These sacred grounds provide the stage for the many roles assumed by the actors in the Zulu religious drama. What is particularly interesting about these roles is that they identify who the leaders and specialists in the Zulu community are. An examination of them will show how political, social, and religious functions in Zulu society overlap and interact with each other. For example, the headman of the kraal leads the rituals for the ancestors, is responsible for decisions that affect the everyday lives of its inhabitants, and maintains the correct relationships between every person in the village.

Of the many roles enacted by the Zulu, eight have a particularly important place in their religious practice. These are those of headman/priest, **diviner**, **herbalist**, patient, **heaven-herd**, supplicant, sorcerer, and witch.

The headman of each Zulu kraal is the chief official of the village and also that person most directly responsible for the performance of the ritual acts expected of all Zulu, especially those that address the ancestors. His role is, therefore, political, social, and religious in nature. He is called **umnumzane**. Religiously, he represents the people of the kraal to the ancestors and the ancestors of the headman's lineage to the people. This position is of great ritual significance in the religious world of the Zulu because the ancestors are a focal point of their religion. The ancestors have great power, and they act for the good or ill of the villagers. These ancestors require reverence and devotion, and the umnumzane ensures that both in attitude and in act the members of the community for which he is responsible perform their religious duty. Whether it be birth, marriage, or death, the headman will be involved in some manner, and it is in the kraal that such acts will be performed.

Divination, the ritual acts performed to diagnose the reason for a misfortune or the means to the solution of some human problem, is widespread throughout Africa. As we shall see, it has achieved a highly systematic and intricate character among the Yoruba. Divination is an important activity among the Zulu, and the role of the diviner is widespread in Zulu society.

One needs a special calling from the ancestral spirits in order to become a diviner. Though anyone can become a diviner, this is a vocation in Zulu society that is most often assumed by women. The Zulu regard the ancestors as the ones who do the calling. Such a calling takes a special form. Often it comes in the form of a vision or a dream. Such a visitation is often accompanied by aches, pains, or other bodily disorders. The calling also involves special training under an experienced diviner; divining is not regarded as a casual affair, for identifying the cause of a problem takes great skill.

Diviners find the cause of a problem; herbalists prescribe the cure. Although most Zulu know something about herbs and other kinds of medicines, and many Zulu are experts in the knowledge of and prescription of particular medicines, there are Zulu who are specialists in medicine and who have a wide range of medical knowledge. Such a Zulu specialist is known as an **izinyanga ze-mithi**, a specialist in medicine, or **izinyanga zokwelapha**, a specialist in healing.

Whereas most diviners are women, most herbalists are men. Knowledge of medicine is usually handed down from father to son. But as I have already indicated, there is widespread knowledge of medicine, and particular people in the community will have knowledge of special medicines for special purposes.

One of the most interesting features of Zulu medicine is that it is not a completely traditional system. By this I mean that the izinyanga is in constant search for new and more effective medicines, and records show that medicines introduced by Westerners have been enthusiastically received and have become part of the medical repertoire. Thus, though it has a strong traditional base, Zulu medicine is a flexible system that has proven to be quite open to new knowledge.

Whereas the roles of headman/priest, diviner, and herbalist are formal and public roles, that of patient, the user of medicine, is an informal and private one. Because of the flexibility of Zulu medicine both with regard to the practitioner and to the materials used, many of the people are self prescribers. This includes the ability to diagnose and cure one's own illness. Thus the patient may either consult a herbalist, or engage in self-prescription; in either case there is a direct relationship between the patient and the power of medicine. Strictly speaking, mediation on the part of the herbalist is not necessary to tap that power.

The **izinyanga zezulu**, the specialists in matters having to do with the sky—for example, thunderstorms and lightning—have a very important ritual role to play in the Zulu religious drama. These individuals are responsible for "herding" the thunderstorms that frequent Zululand, and they are known, therefore, as "heaven-herds." It should be remembered that cattle are of fundamental importance to the Zulu, and therefore the imagery of cattle and the activities associated with cattle occur quite frequently. (The role of the heaven-herd is always occupied by a Zulu male because of the close association between men and cattle.)

Heaven-herding is a vocation; it is a role to which a man is called in a special way by the **God of the Sky**: for example, the individual might receive a special sign, perhaps an especially close encounter with a bolt of lightning, that will convince him that the God of the Sky has chosen him for this work. The candidate for the role will then go through a period of apprenticeship with an experienced heaven-herd. Part of his initiation will be having special cuts made on his face by an experienced heaven-herd. This is a special, permanent marking of the face called scarification.

What is special about the role of the heaven-herd is that he will have a ritual relationship with the God of the Sky instead of the ancestors. The weather is under the control of the God of the Sky; it is he who sends the lightning and the wind and the rain. So the job of the heaven-herd is to repel or divert the approaching storm and to mitigate its effects. Just like the **umfaan**, the young lad who herds the cattle to their special grazing spots, the heaven-herd guides the weather for human benefit.

Most of Zulu religious life centers upon reverence for the ancestors and the ritual obligations associated with these revered predecessors. But occasions do arise when it is thought necessary for special acts to be performed over which the ancestors have no control or into which the ancestors have given no indication that they care to intrude. The Zulu supplicant, that is, anyone who communes directly with the God of the Sky, will know that, in such a situation of dire need, help is possible from the God of the Sky. The God of the Sky is communicated with only in such special situations, when neither the headman/priest nor the diviner nor the herbalist have demonstrated an ability to help. Only then are special acts of supplication to the God of the Sky in order. Such communication with the God of the Sky will take place on those hills known by the Zulu supplicant to be arenas for an encounter with him. It should be noted, then, that what the heaven-herd and the supplicant have in common is a special ritual location—the hills of God, on which to worship him.

Any Zulu can be a sorcerer. In other words, the role of the sorcerer is general; no one person or set of persons is always and consistently a sorcerer. The reason is that **sorcery** depends upon the situation; a special grievance has to arise for one Zulu to feel that the occasion is ripe for the expression of the grievance. This angered individual, the one with the grievance, will consult with either a diviner or a herbalist. A diviner is the likely consultant if it is the cause of the problem that needs clarification. Of course, if the diviner traffics in medicine then two jobs can be done at the same time. If the aggrieved person is convinced of the cause but requires the means of sorcery, he or she will consult a herbalist with knowledge of those medicines that can have the desired effect.

To engage in sorcery is to have access to medicinal and spiritual power and to use such powers for destructive ends. The intent of the sorcerer is to harm by the straightforward means made available through the knowledge provided by the herbalist and the diviner. And the motive is often revenge. Anyone with a knowledge of medicine can perform sorcery. One simply devises the techniques to use its power (**amandla**) for evil ends.

There is nothing straightforward about the role of the witch in the Zulu religious world. First of all, no one really knows who the witches are. The role of witch is completely private. It is also completely secret. It is important to note this secrecy, because the headman/priest, the heaven-herd, the diviner, and the herbalist are open, traditionally prescribed, and public roles. But the maker of witchcraft is that unknown individual, almost always considered to be a woman, who misuses valid and good power for invalid and evil ends. Witchcraft is a threat to public order, an unbearable strain on traditional social organization, a challenge to revered tradition. Witches derive their power from, and base their operations in, a shadowy world that is neither that of the ancestors nor that of the God of the Sky. And their purpose is the destruction of what is good, especially those processes that create and enhance life. The **abathakati** (witch) is the specialist in evil, the one who twists the system with its centers of power for destructive purposes.

Failure to show due reverence for the ancestors may result in sickness and suffering; the consequences of witchcraft are destruction and death. Such destruction and death comes neither from the God of the Sky nor from the ancestors nor from medicine. Nor does it come even from sorcery, which is the straightforward expression of anger due to justifiable grievances. It comes from the twisted use of power for evil ends.

Any woman can become a witch; she becomes one through the experience of possession. It is possible, however, for a Zulu to be a witch without even knowing it. This cannot be said of any other role in Zulu society. Witches are regarded as having superhuman properties; they can fly at night, can become invisible, and can act on others at a distance. Witches also have a relationship to special kinds of snakes, and the presence of a snake of a certain kind is a clue to the operation of witchcraft.

Understanding the nature and function of these eight roles advances our knowledge of the world view of the Zulu and leads us to questions about the centers of power around which they revolve.

We now have two locations for the Zulu religious drama, the kraal and specially designated unoccupied hills. We have the roles played by those enacting the drama: the headman/priest, the diviner, the herbalist, the heaven-herd, the supplicant, the patient, the sorcerer, and the witch. What is the drama about? It is about the use and misuse of power, amandla. But what is power for the Zulu, and how is such power expressed?

Power is that which is capable of bringing about a change in a situation, an alteration of a status, a variation in a condition. For the Zulu there are three legitimate elements that are capable of exerting power in this sense. These sources of power are the ancestors, the God of the Sky, and **medicine**. As we have already seen in our discussion of witchcraft, there is also evil power. Evil power is the misuse of power for destructive ends. Legitimate power sustains life in an orderly, customary fashion. When judgment is necessary it follows from the acknowledged structure of the Zulu religious world. Illegitimate power destroys life. It introduces disorder, disrupts human relationships, unleashes vengeance, and destroys the equilibrium that characterizes the intricate balances of everyday Zulu life.

The role of ritual is to maintain and enhance the relationships the Zulu have to the powers of life. The following sections describe the Zulu conceptions of each of these powers in more detail.

The ancestral spirits variously known as the **amalozi, amakhosi**, or **amathonga**, are of fundamental significance for the

Zulu. They are the departed souls of the deceased. Although they are regarded as having gone to abide in the earth, they continue to have a relationship with those still living in the kraal. They are regarded as positive, constructive, and creative presences. They are also capable of meting out punishment when they have been wronged or ignored. Veneration is their due. Failure to show proper respect to them invites misfortune, proper veneration ensures benefit. The ancestors, therefore, are powers for either good or ill. When such power is judgmental it is not regarded as destructive, for its purpose it to maintain traditional relationships. For an ancestor to bring misfortune on a living member of the kraal is viewed as a legitimate expression of wrath attributable to the failure of one or more living members of the kraal to do their duty.

The Zulu make a distinction among ancestors. Zulu society is patrilineal, that is, authority and inheritance proceed through the male line from father to son. The important ancestors for a kraal are male ancestors, particularly the former headman/priest. Of course the great chiefs of the Zulu nation are also very important ancestors, and there will be occasions when they are addressed by praise songs and appealed to for help.

The ancestors are regarded as living in or under the earth. They are also identified with the earth. But they have a particular association with two places in the kraal, the umsamo and the cattle kraal, especially that place in the cattle kraal where the important religious rituals are performed. They are constantly watching over the activities of their descendants. (see Figure 1.)

The Zulu word for the sky is izulu. It is clear, therefore, that the Zulu have a religious relationship to the sky as well as to the earth, the abode of the ancestors. In fact, the Zulu trace their ancestry to an act of creation by the God of the Sky. The God of the Sky, **Inkosi Yezulu** (literally, "chief of the sky"), also has a special name Umvelingqangi, which means "that which appeared first." It also implies "the first of twins." Presumably the other twin is the earth. The God of the Sky is male, father; the earth is female, mother. Upon death the ancestors return to mother. Only in special circumstances do people go to be with Umvelingqangi.

The God of the Sky and the earth are regarded as having brought forth **Abantu** ("the people"). But the view of the origin of the abantu is a complicated one. First, the Zulu do believe that the Amazulu (the Zulu people) come from the God of the Sky; the God of the Sky sent down through a hole in the dome of the sky a male still attached to an umbilical cord. Then a reed was used to cut the umbilical cord. Second, the Zulu also say that humankind came from the breaking off of reeds. These two accounts might reflect two traditions, now merged, or they might reflect a distinction between the origins of the Zulu and the origins of all people, or it might indicate that the creation of the first man by the God of the Sky is a later story. Some scholars argue that it is a later story developed under the influence of the Christian missionaries.

What is interesting is that both the God of the Sky and the ancestors are referred to as *inkosi* by the Zulu. But the ancestors are usually referred to as a group, the *amakosi*, whereas the singular, *inkosi*, refers to the God of the Sky. Yet the ancestors are clearly referred to as people of the earth. It is probable that the God of the Sky is not a later addition but has been present for a long time in the religious system of the Zulu. But the role of the High God has been misunderstood and misinterpreted. Clearly, in the earliest accounts recorded by travelers and missionaries, he appears but is confused with Unkulunkulu, the first man, who also had a creator-like role in establishing the first people.

The God of the Sky has praise names associated with him.[1] Praise names (**isibongo**) and the highly stylized poetry associated with praise names are of fundamental importance in Zulu life. All important personages in the history of the Zulu people have praise names associated with them, and praise poems are sung at important occasions. The fact of Umvelingqangi having praise names is important proof of his traditional and continuing importance in the Zulu religious world.

Praise is important in Zulu social relations, and the ceremonial use of praise names is one very important method the Zulu use to recapitulate their history. In fact there are transcriptions of the isibongo of all the Zulu kings back to King Zulu himself. These praise poems are an important source of historical information and clearly reflect the Zulu attitudes toward their past leaders. They also express reverence and respect for all sources of power, whether these be ancestors or the High God.

As we have already indicated, it is unusual for a Zulu to approach the God of the Sky; it is the ancestors who are most frequently addressed. But there do arise conditions of dire need, both for individuals and for groups—for example, a severe drought—and on such occasions, when neither medicine nor the ancestors have been effective in alleviating a bad situation, the Zulu will address the God of the Sky, as supplicants. Then the Zulu will take to the hills, there to commune with Umvelingqangi in isolation from the world of the kraal and the ancestors occupying it.

The God of the Sky has a special relationship with thunder and lightning. Storms are his direct acts. Should a person be killed by lightning, he or she is regarded as having been taken by Umvelingqangi. Such people do not become ancestors. They do not reside under the earth, are not present in any of their usual locations; in fact, they are to be buried as close as possible to where they were taken, and they are not ever to be talked about. They are "with the God of the Sky." Because of this, no mourning for them is encouraged or permitted. Whereas the ancestors have gone down, the people killed by lightning have gone up.

The third type of power acknowledged by the Zulu is the power of medicine. The power of medicine is neither the power of the ancestors nor the power of the God of the Sky; it has its own power. One might almost say that medicine represents a system of its own. The God of the Sky, the ancestors, and medicine can each act for the good or ill of people. All are capable of bringing about change in a situation, alteration of a status, variation of a condition.

All three powers are capable of treating illness, but it is the particular nature of medicine to maintain or restore health, although it can be misused in acts of sorcery. The point to remember is that medicine does not depend upon either the power of Umvelingqangi or the ancestors for its efficacy. It stands on its own, and its amandla can be added to by new knowledge.

Evil power is negative and destructive. It is not an independent, autonomous power as are the God of the Sky, the ancestors, and medicine; it derives its influence from these three positive elements in the Zulu religious world. The three positive elements maintain and enhance and ensure normal, traditional relationships. Abathakatha is the misuse of positive power for destructive ends. As such it is a serious and constant threat to the social fabric. Those who manipulate this evil power tamper with established objects, actions, and roles. When the three other sources of power are expressed, legitimate action occurs even if its consequences entail pain, suffering, and death, for in such instances there has been failure to perform an appropriate obligation. To use witchcraft is to participate in the shadowy world of evil and to go outside the bounds of all that is good and right and prescribed. Whereas the practitioners of medicine are known and public, the practitioners of evil are hidden from view. Whereas the sorcerer will misuse the

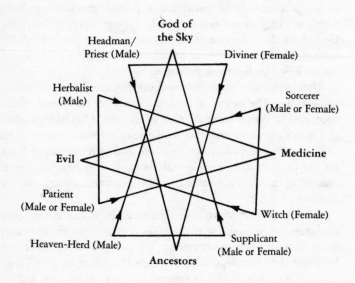

Figure 2

amandla of medicine for bad ends, the witch will twist the entire fabric of the system for destructive purposes and introduce death into the world.

We now know who the practitioners of the various religious roles are, and we know the various expressions of power in the Zulu religious world. The question is, How does the system work? How do those who assume the roles that they do in the Zulu religious world relate themselves to the sources of power?

First I will summarize with a diagram what we have seen thus far.

This diagram uses a set of interlocking triangles to represent the relationships that hold in Zulu religion between the ritual roles and sources of power. The base of each triangle symbolizes the observable, ritual aspect of Zulu religion. The apex of each triangle indicates the power each role is designed to tap.

There are four triangles, which represent the four powers (the God of the Sky, the ancestors, medicine, and evil) and the four sets of roles that can be discerned in Zulu religion. The four triangles are interlocked to emphasize the interconnectedness of the various roles with each other and with the sources of power.

In the case of the God of the Sky, it is the heaven-herd and the supplicant who perform the ritual actions necessary to provide the power available from that source. In the case of the ancestors, it is the headman/priest and the diviner who are responsible for the rites that establish and maintain the right relationship with these sources of power. In the case of medicine, it is the herbalist and the patient who have the knowledge and perform the deeds necessary to derive the healing and the protection available from this source. In the case of evil, it is the sorcerer and the witch who have the knowledge and intent to distort and twist the power generally available from the other sources for destructive ends.

Such a diagram describes graphically roles and relationships that the Zulu believe to be important, real, and effective; it permits us to organize the information available from the observers of Zulu life as well as from the Zulu themselves and to ask further questions.

I now propose to show how particular events in Zulu life can be seen as expressing the Zulu religous system in action. We shall see how the various roles in the religious system function in the everyday life of the Zulu, especially in those important events understood as stages on life's way.

Consider the following situation: the headman of a particular Zulu kraal has died in the prime of life of an unexpected illness. How will the religious system come into play? Who will do what?

If the members of the Zulu kraal still follow the traditional Zulu ways, there are a number of rituals that will be performed. First, the body of the deceased headman will be prepared. This will involve the ritual washing of his face, the shaving of his head (the hair will be retained and buried with him), and the manipulation of his body into a sitting position with his knees drawn up to his chin. Then his body will be bound in oxhide or, if it is not available, in a blanket and placed against one of the poles supporting the hut, where it will then be shielded from view by a covering of some sort. These actions will be performed under the supervision of the new headman/priest, the first son of the deceased leader.[2]

After these initial acts a grave will be dug near the main hut of the kraal by the first son. The burial will occur at night. In recent times this aspect of the ritual has not always been adhered to except in the case of especially distinguished figures. The less frequent adherence is due to the influence of Christianity which usually performs burials during the day. When the body is placed in the grave near the main hut, it is positioned so that the head of the body faces the hut. During these activities there will have been the sounds of wailing and lamenting; the actual funeral procession takes place in complete silence.

For a month after the burial, the behavior required of everyone in the kraal is quite specific. There can be no work. There is quiet and inactivity. No sexual activity is permitted during this monthlong period of mourning.

The event of death in a Zulu kraal is regarded as a time of great danger for everyone. This means that everyone must be protected from the powers that have caused the death. In the situation we are discussing, the death is untimely. Such deaths will either be regarded by the members of the kraal as punishment from the ancestors for failure to perform some obligation to them or for having offended them in some way or may be regarded as having been caused by an act of either sorcery or witchcraft. The point is that, although there may have already developed some suspicion among the mourners about the possible cause, no one knows yet exactly why the death has occurred. It is important, therefore, for the people to find out why. It is also important for the survivors to avoid further problems. Two of the roles we have described will therefore come into play; that of the diviner and that of the herbalist or specialist in medicine. It will be the diviner's obligation to identify the cause of the untimely death and the herbalist's to provide the medicines that will protect the villagers. The diviner's activities will stretch over a considerable period; those of the herbalist are more immediate.

Immediately after the headman has been buried, the people of the kraal will begin taking medicines as a protective device. As we have already found, medicine has its own power and is not reduceable to the other powers in the Zulu religious world. Either the herbalist will prescribe the appropriate medicines to take or, because knowledge of medicine is quite widespread in the Zulu community, there will be self-prescription. This act of taking medicine is so important that no one from the affected kraal is permitted to leave it or to communicate with people in other kraals until the medical treatment has occurred. Some of the medicine will be placed on the umsamo, and some of it will also be used to treat the cattle.

Having taken the medicines that will provide the strength and protection necessary in such a dangerous situation, the people will then perform other important ritual acts. There will be a ritual washing in the closest stream, the ritual slaughter of an animal such as a goat, and the purification of the hut of the deceased headman. The slaughter of the goat is not regarded as a sacrifice to the ancestors but as yet another form of medicine to protect the survivors from danger. The goat, in fact, is called **imbuzi yamakhubalo**, "the goat of medicine."

The general period of mourning lasts for a month, but this period does not apply to the widow of the deceased headman, for whom the period of mourning is a year.

The month-long period of mourning for all but the closest relatives comes to an end with the **ihlambo** ceremony. *Ihlambo* means "the washing of spears" of all the men associated with the kraal. In actual practice the ritual is more complicated than the washing of the spears, for both the men and the women of the village are expected to perform those acts that signal the end of the period of mourning. In practice, the men ritually wash their spears and the women ritually wash their hoes. They are "washed," however, not with water but with action. The men wash their spears by going on a hunt and the women, by hoeing in the fields. After these religious acts have been performed, the implements are regarded as having been cleaned, and the people are free to return to their normal patterns of living. But one more ritual has to be accomplished during the ihlambo; the praises of the departed headman must be sung, an animal must be sacrificed, and there must be a final taking of medicine.

Now the widow of the headman is alone in the continuation of mourning for the rest of the year. To symbolize her mourning, she will wear an *intambo* (a grass headband), refrain from sexual relations, and live a life of great circumspection. At the end of the year-long period of mourning, she will be ritually purified with the appropriate medicines and then be ready either for marriage to one of the brothers of the deceased or for the journey back to her parents' kraal.

And now the kraal is ready for the final ritual, the **ukubuyisa idlozi**, "the bringing home of the ancestor." All this time the deceased headman has been in an "in-between" state, neither here nor there. He is now ready to be joined with the other ancestors by being brought home, for the ancestors though living in an "underworld" also live right in the kraal. The deceased headman must, therefore, be brought back to his rightful place among the living, there to continue to exert his influence collectively with the amakhosi, the group of ancestors. His presence in the umsamo, in the doorways, in the cattle kraal, and in the hearts and minds of the people needs to be ensured. Failure to perform the ukubuyisa idlozi would create danger for all members of the kraal. It clearly would be treated by the ancestors as an insult.

The ukubuyisa is a festive occasion involving joy, feasting, and fellowship. A special ox is sacrificed, and other animals are also killed. Special portions of the ox are placed on the umsamo; other portions are ritually burned; and the rest remains in the hut of the deceased headman. The following day all of the ox is eaten; none of it can be left over or removed from the kraal. The other meat and food prepared can be removed or given as gifts to members of other kraals. The ancestor may be guided to the umsamo from the grave site by the new headman/priest, the chief son of the former headman/priest, by making marks with twigs. At the umsamo the idlozi (ancestor) may be called upon to return to his rightful place. This will be the first time that the ancestor is addressed and praised along with the other ancestors. For it is now right and good to show him reverence and respect and to treat him as a source of power for good or ill. And now the chief son is ready to assume completely the role of headman/priest.

It should be clear from the description of the death of the head-man/priest and the actions performed by the members of the kraal that key elements of the religious system are at work. Special places have provided the ritual ground for religious actions, special roles have come into play, and special powers have been acknowledged. The kraal provides the scene for the burial rites and the burial plot. And within the kraal the umsamo assumes special importance as one place where the ancestors are communicated with. There are also special roles at work, those of the headman/priest, the diviner, and the herbalist. And special powers are acknowledged, the pow-er of evil that has caused the death because of the activities of witchcraft, the power of medicine that prevents the danger from spreading, the power of the ancestors who maintain the people and situation in balance and who receive the deceased into their world. This description has given us the occasion to examine some of the details of a rite of passage, in this case from the everyday world to the world of the ancestors. It also provides the opportunity to dis-cuss other rites of passage practiced by the Zulu, under the rubric of the stages on life's way.

Let us now consider the new headman/priest to whom the mantle of leadership has passed. How did he achieve this promi-nent position? What has been his career? What stages did he have to pass through in order to arrive at his present position? We shall give him a name, Bhudaza, and trace the orderly progression of his life starting from the time of his birth.[3]

From the moment his mother recognized that she was preg-nant, Bhudaza was part of a religious world. When she felt his first stirrings, his mother who was to give him birth immediately re-garded herself as being in a dangerous situation. The powers spelled potential danger for the developing child, and precautions had to be taken to protect the mother and her coming child from the wrath of the ancestors and the acts of sorcerers and witches. She called upon the knowledge of the herbalist to prescribe the right protective medicines and began eating only those foods ritually permitted.

When the time came for Bhudaza's delivery, his mother was attended by the old women of the kraal in their capacity as midwives. She knew that her first son's birth would be auspicious, because before his birth she saw an ancestor in the form of a snake.

As soon as Bhudaza was born he was taken to the umsamo; a special hole was dug in this sacred place, and he was bathed in the hole. The water used in the bathing was treated with medicine, and his umbilical cord was buried in the hole in the umsamo. Cattle, and the milk of cattle, are of great religious significance, and so, before he was permitted to drink his mother's milk, he was fed cows' milk or *amasi*, the specially treated curds of milk. The religious significance lay in the fact that Zulu identity is intimately connected with the imagery of cattle.

Because medicine has a power of its own, the first few days after his birth he was treated again with medicines, and because of the danger of the wrath of his ancestors and the powers of sorcery and witchcraft, he and his mother were isolated. The period of isolation was brought to an end by the ritual purification of the mother. This involved taking medicine prescribed by the herbalist.

Only then was the father permitted to see the child. The father's first ritual act was to sacrifice an ox to the ancestors. This was an act of both thanksgiving and precaution. The baby was then ready to be named. His name involved a great deal of careful thought and consultation, and when it was decided upon, this name was either based upon some significant event or referred to some ancestor. In this case the name Bhudaza was chosen because it figures prominently in a praise song to Macingwane, son of Lubhoko of the Chunu clan, and Bhudaza was a new member of that clan.

Sometime before puberty Bhudaza had his ears pierced. A special ceremony marked this occasion, which occurred either at the appearance of the new moon or when the moon was full.

Isolation or seclusion is always used to mark transition, and so the night before the **qhumbaza** Bhudaza was isolated. On the day of the ritual, which is performed either by a herbalist or an experienced ear-piercer in the kraal, a sacrifice of a male animal was performed. His father, the headman/priest, went to the um-samo with special cuts of the sacrificial animal, and there he thanked the ancestors for having given him a first son and for keeping him safe to that day. It is then that the operation on his ears was performed at the entrance to the cattle kraal, the abode of the ancestors.

The next important event in Bhudaza's life was the **thomba** ceremony, which marks the onset of puberty. Every Zulu boy is taught to watch for the sign that will mark the next significant event in his life, namely, his first nocturnal emission.

The morning after this sexual event, long before the sun had risen, Bhudaza took the cattle from the kraal, and perhaps even the cattle from neighboring kraals, and hid them in a place difficult to find. Once the cattle were hidden he ritually bathed in the closest stream and then waited for his agemates to come and find him.

The disappearance of the cattle alerted everyone in his kraal to the significance of the event, and the search for the missing cattle and boy commenced. While the search was in progress Bhudaza's father began to make preparations for the ritual events to follow. The most important of these was the preparation of medicines. When the boy and the cattle were discovered, they were driven back into the cattle kraal. After the father welcomed him and treated him with medicine, he was taken to one of the huts and told to sit right in the umsamo. He would have been in such close proximity to this sacred place at only one other time, at the ritual bathing attending his birth. The umsamo at all other times is strictly off limits; it is sacred space not to be violated. As Bhudaza sat in the umsamo area of the hut he was covered with a screen to shield him from view. Only his agemates were permitted to visit with him during this inbetween period. If he left the hut at all, it would have been with great circumspection; under no conditions was he permitted to see or come into contact with women.

When Bhudaza had been driven back to the kraal his father had set aside the special day for the puberty feast. When that day arrived, the boy Bhudaza was led from his place of seclusion to the cattle kraal. There an ox was sacrificed, isibongo (praise poems) were sung to the ancestors, and he was treated with medicines. Then offerings were made to the ancestors by the headman/priest in the umsamo, and the boy was led back to the hut. After a further addressing of the ancestors, and before the feast began, he was taken by his agemates to the river and ritually bathed, his old garments were removed and destroyed, and he was given new clothes. He was also given a new name. He now had two names: his birth name, Bhudaza, and the name Mdingi given to him by his agemates.

Not only were his old clothes destroyed but also the screen that had shielded him from view. In his new finery Bhudaza and his agemates then started to dance. At first the boy followed the others, but gradually he assumed the role of the leader of the dance. The spirit of the dance took over, and soon the entire assembly was dancing and feasting.

On the evening of the next day Bhudaza went again to the umsamo where, as he communicated with his ancestors, he ate meat from the sacrificial ox that had been specially treated with medicine. He was now ready for the next stage of his life.

Before its sovereignty was destroyed by the combined forces of British colonialism and the developing white South African state, the Zulu kingdom was armed with numerous regiments. The great Zulu chief Shaka had devised a plan for forming efficient, well-disciplined regiments to be the military arm of the new Zulu kingdom. An important stage in the career of the young Zulu male was induction into one of these regiments, which occurred within a year or two after the thomba ritual. Even though this ritual induction into the regiment is fast disappearing today, the concept still survives. If Bhudaza were living in the time of the full flower of the Zulu nation he would be so inducted.

The first part of the **ukubuthwa** or "grouping-up" ritual consisted of an ordeal, undergoing harsh treatment at the hands of experienced members of the regiment, hard work, ritual combat, and serious competition among those grouping up together.

The second part consisted of instruction. During this stage of the initiation ceremony, Bhudaza learned the rules of regimental life—especially obedience and respect for authority, abstinence from sexual relations with women during the induction period, and the eating of special foods meant to strengthen the inductees.

Young Zulu woman. Photograph by the author.

During the third part of the induction ceremony the regiment to which Bhudaza was giving his allegiance received its name. This naming was the prerogative of the king only. After the king announced the name, a ritual chanting of important isibongo, or praise names, took place accompanied by dancing.

The fourth part of the ritual was the presentation of the weapons of war. These assegais, or spears, after being given to each member of the regiment, were then presented to the headman of the district in which each young man lived, there to remain until being called upon to be used in battle.

After Bhudaza had completed his induction or grouping up into his regiment he returned to his kraal where he was greeted joyously by his father. A special ox was sacrificed, the ancestors were praised, and there was general feasting and merrymaking. In the heyday of the Zulu kingdom such an induction could last as long as six months depending upon the king's decision. It could also be little more than a week or two.

Bhudaza was now ready for marriage. His life had changed. Up until this point he was an umfaan, a boy whose main responsibility was the herding of the cattle of the kraal. Now he was released from such duties and could begin the joyful time of courting. As with every other stage of his life, this period of courtship and marriage involved religious activity for the appropriation of power. One important source of power is, of course, medicine, and so Bhudaza used medicine to aid him in his search for a wife. Love potions would give him the kind of power to attract the right maiden.

Besides taking love potions, Bhudaza also wore the **kehla**, or headring, as a special religious symbol of the imminence of his marriage. And when he had found a wife, marriage plans were put into effect. Such plans involved a number of actions. The first of these is known as *lobola*. Lobola is the practice of transferring cattle from his kraal to that of his future wife. Rather than being a bride price, this was regarded as a protective measure on the part of both families. The second activity for Bhudaza was receiving the consent of his future wife's older sisters and her parents. Complex negotiations between the two kraals then ensued. Finally, after many intricate maneuvers, his bride arrived at his kraal for the wedding activities.

The most important of the wedding rituals was the exchange of gifts between the two kraals involved in the wedding. Bhudaza's bride, upon her arrival with her family, began to sing a special song to her ancestors. Shortly thereafter, his mother and the other wives of his father began to sing a song also. Slowly two groups formed on each side of the cattle kraal. The bridal party occupied the ground on the right side of the cattle kraal and the bridegroom's

Dancing and drumming at a Zulu wedding. Photograph by Brian Jones.

party was on the left side. The two sides sang to each other. They also shouted, and played the drums. This activity continued through the night.

The next day the bridal party left the kraal, the bride was secluded, and the bridal party dressed for the occasion. After a while they returned to the kraal and there was more dancing. Then the *umbeka* beast—usually an ox—which represents the ancestors of the bride in her new home, was guided to a position between the two wedding parties. The father of the bride addressed the ancestors, requesting them to accept the bride in her new status. Bhudaza's uncle addressed the ancestors of his kraal, apologized for the loss of cattle to the bride's kraal, but informed them of the exchange of these cattle for a bride and the umbeka beast. Then the cattle belonging to Bhudaza's father were paraded before the assembled people.

After this there was a general celebration and feast. The bride, after a brief seclusion, returned to the kraal of the groom. The *umqholiso* ox, the wedding ox to be sacrificed to the ancestors, was killed, and the gall of the ox was poured over the bride. The ancestors have a particular liking for gall, and this act associated the bride with the ancestors of Bhudaza. The sacrificed ox was eaten by both families, and the bride then entered Bhudaza's hut. That night the bride and groom consummated their marriage.

On the following day the ceremony of the beads took place. Bhudaza had to choose a bead from the left hand of his wife. His wife concealed the beads from him by rolling them around in her hand. The beads were black, red, and white in color. The groom hoped for a white bead as this would signal a good marriage. (If it were red she would not be a virgin, and if black it would indicate that she had been promiscuous.) Then the bride handed out articles that she herself had made for her new relatives. The bride was then anointed with fat by her mother-in-law, and she then donned the standard dress of a married woman.

On the fourth morning of the wedding, the bride ritually cleaned the kraal of the bridegroom's family, helped by her friends, who then left for their own villages. Only one ritual act remained: the bride had to cut a piece of cow dung with a knife before she could begin to eat the regular food of her new kraal.

The bride had now left the home of her ancestors and taken up a new dwelling with the ancestors of her husband. While Bhudaza had simply changed from an unmarried to a married man, his wife had also changed from one ancestral abode to another, a much more radical change, and one quite capable of introducing dangerous powers into both situations. Great care and circumspection was, therefore, required on her part. This meant living strictly according to the obligations of a new wife in a new situation. Especially significant was the requirement that she cover her face as she moved about the kraal. Failure to cover her face would have indicated a lack of reverence for the ancestors present there and could have brought upon her and everyone in the kraal the ancestors' anger. After a few months she was permitted to remove this sign of respect. Now Bhudaza and his new wife would look forward to the birth of their first child. If this child were a son, he would automatically become the heir, and the cycle with which we began this account of the stages on life's way would begin again. At Bhudaza's death the same rituals that were performed for his father would be performed for him, and the life cycle would be complete.

In our own society we are usually quite aware of when our behavior is religious and when it is not. We know the difference between praising the cook for her excellent apple pie and praising God for her mercies, the difference between raising the flag and raising the host. Such distinctions are usually easy to make, because we have been taught to make them from an early age. But when we study another society we discover that such distinctions are not obvious at all. It is much more difficult to make such a distinction when talking about the Zulu. Almost every act that a Zulu performs is religious. Perhaps a simpler way to put it is that the way the Zulu live their lives is organized religiously. This means that the stages on life's way are invested with significance; there are appropriate and inappropriate forms of action. The new bride appropriately covers her head in the presence of her husband's ancestors; not to do so is to show disrespect. But this religious system also changes. At one time, the bridegroom chose the hidden bead from the bride's hand. But if he did not get the white one, it was pretty traumatic. Today the groom often hits the beads out of her hand and grabs the white one, thus ensuring the right outcome. The point is that the Zulu religious system has changed over the last hundred and fifty years. One of the reasons for the change has been the encounter with the cultures of the West, which includes such notions as the difference between religious and nonreligious action. But what is most impressive is the ability of the Zulu religious system to deal with new situations and ideas in a flexible and creative manner. The belief in the power of the ancestors has not changed, but under the influence of Western religions such as Christianity, Islam, and even Indian religions (for there are many Indians living in the province of Natal), elements of the Zulu religious system have been given increased significance.

The belief in the God of the Sky is a very old Zulu belief. But until the encounter with other religions, there never had been much ritual action associated with this source of power. With the incursion of Christianity, and especially with the introduction of the **Zionist** church and other new religions into Zulu life, a much greater emphasis has been placed by some Zulu on communication with the God of the Sky. So the special hilltops associated with his worship are scenes of increasing activity as the influence of the Zionist and other independent churches grows. The God of the Sky, though an important presence and source of power in the Zulu religious world, has never been in the forefront of religious attention. But the very acknowledgement of such a power has made it possible for the Zulu to respond to both internal and external challenges to their religious system. Such is its flexibility.

Another example of flexibility is the power of medicine. Traditional medicine is still practiced in Zululand to this day, but Western medicines are slowly being added to—not replacing—such traditional medicines. Clearly, whatever medicine is used is treated as a source of more than physical and chemical changes, for medicine is an independent source of healing power, where healing involves more than purely physical well-being.

Yet another example of the flexibility of the religious system can be seen in the ritual actions of women. Zulu society is patrilineal in organization. In practical terms this means the dominance of males in the social and religious order. Women nevertheless have significant areas for religious action. Some of these have already been noted. For example, though the headman/priest is the main conduit to and the main representative of the ancestors, the woman diviner also has access to them through the ritual activity of divination. Zulu certainly have a healthy respect for witchcraft and sorcery, and the role of women in these activities is thought to be prominent. But there are specific important rituals that are the exclusive province of women.

In the diagram of the religious world in Figure 2 there is one element missing, namely, the Princess of the Sky. Although the ancestors and the God of the Sky receive the most attention, the religious system is flexible enough to provide room for a ritual role for women. Nowhere is this role clearer than in the relationship between women and Inkosazana, the Princess of the Sky. The Princess has a number of significant features that contribute to the overall complexity of the religious system. She is associated with both virginity and fertility of all creatures. But most significantly, she is capable of instituting rules of behavior and ritual action that are distinct from those of both the God of the Sky and the ancestors. For example, the herding of cattle is an activity confined to young men. But under the instructions of the Princess of the Sky, young women, clothed like men, do engage in this activity. This is a clear example of role reversal in which the power normally associated with one religious role is transferred, ritually, to another.

The Princess of the Sky is also capable of acting as a mediator between the people and the God of the Sky. Under one transformation of the religious system, it is the Princess rather than the heaven-herd who persuades the God of the Sky to send rain.

The location for the appearances and revelations of the Princess is never the kraal but always specific hills or mountains. When communication takes place between her and young women, these women herd some cattle into the hills and there perform a ritual to the Princess.

What is interesting about all of this is that it shows that the religious system of the Zulu has resources within itself to handle the inevitable tensions that arise in a system that so emphasizes the role of the male. In fact, the Princess can be quite dangerous to Zulu men, and she is neither to be approached nor seen by them. She also provides avenues of information to women that otherwise would be closed to them.

What is also clear is that the presence of this creative and responsive capacity in the religious system of the Zulu makes the system capable of dealing with new situations as they arise. This responsive and creative capacity we now turn to.

Transformations of the Religious System

No religious systems are static. They change in various ways. In fact religious systems are very flexible, capable of expressing themselves in novel ways in new settings. The reader will remember that the Zulu kraal was the primary locus of religious action, but the unoccupied hills also played an important role in Zulu religious life. The kraal has a direct relationship to the ancestors; the hills have a direct relationship with the God of the Sky. And though the headman/priest is the ritual practitioner responsible for maintaining relationships with the ancestors, the heaven-herd is responsible for communication with the God of the Sky.

But this duality in the religious system points to a very strong tension within it. Under usual conditions the roles of the two ritual practitioners are clearly defined. The headman/priest pays due

*Isaiah Shembe, Zulu
prophet, a creative reli-
gious leader who estab-
lished the AmaNazaretha
Church. Photograph by
Lynn Acutt. Used with
permission of Oxford Uni-
versity Press.*

reverence to the ancestors; the heaven-herd controls the storm by
the power of the High God. Only when dire situations arise will
the members of the Zulu kraal appeal to the God of the Sky.

But the Zulu people have maintained and developed their
identity in the context of a very complex history. The colonial powers made their presence and power increasingly felt in the nineteenth century; Christians began to establish missions among the
Zulu; and the concepts of Western culture began to exert their
influence. Perhaps most importantly, gold was discovered near **Johannesburg** in 1885, and many young Zulu men were recruited
to work in the mines. One of the consequences of the work in the
mines was disruption of traditional Zulu life.

In this setting of change the development of new religious
movements among the Zulu accelerated. Many scholars writing
about the development of these new religious movements have interpreted them as a Zulu reaction to Christian symbols. Such an
interpretation is far too simple; it does not give due credit to the
religious creativity involved and ignores the inherent power of the
Zulu symbols themselves to achieve new forms in new situations.
Given that there is a built-in tension in the Zulu system, it should

not surprise us that these separate elements in tension may undergo a transformation and find new expression under new conditions. We shall see in our discussion of a founder of a new religious movement, one form that such a transformation can take.

Isaiah Shembe was a Zulu prophet (d. 1935) and a creative religious leader who established a large following in Zululand with his church, the amaNazaretha. Shembe combined Zulu and Christian symbols into a new form of religious life; some scholars interpret it as a Zulu form of Christianity. So, for example, Shembe's claim that he received a revelation from Jehovah receives a great deal of attention, as does his exorcism of demons by the power of the Holy Spirit. But the Zulu religious context is clear and cannot be ignored. Shembe received revelations on separate occasions when he had narrowly escaped from being struck by lightning. In the first experience, he had a vision commanding him to cease from immorality. In the second experience, he had a vision of his own death. In the third, he was told to abandon his four wives. In his fourth encounter, his best ox was killed by lightning, and he received severe burns.

In the religious system of the Zulu it is the heaven-herd who receives his call to his ritual role with the God of the Sky by means of a close encounter with lightning. And it is the hills that provide the locus for his religious acts. What is interesting is that when Shembe built his first church kraal it was on top of a hill and was called "The High Place." And one of the first pilgrimages that Shembe led was to Nhlangakazi Mountain in Natal, a mountain that has since become the setting for the New Year festival of the amaNazaretha church.

Both the form and the content of Shembe's experience illustrate that transformation has been at work. There is both a traditional and a new element in these emerging religious systems. The traditional element is the entire set of symbols connected with the God of the Sky: the heaven-herd, the hills, lightning, and the experience of possession or visions or dreams. The new element is the association of these symbols with the imagery provided by Christianity, such as Jehovah, Holy Spirit, and spiritual healing. Shembe also retained, unchanged, many of the other aspects of the Zulu system, such as the practice of sorcery and witchcraft.

In effect what Shembe accomplished was the transformation of the role of the heaven-herd from that of controller of severe weather by the power available from the God of the Sky to that of the prophet of the God of the Sky with a message of healing for the Zulu in their time of suffering. This message from above did not deny the reality and importance of the ancestors or of the power of medicine or of the destructive power of sorcery and witchcraft. If he had adopted such an approach he would have been ignored. But the silent God of the Sky became capable of speaking, capable of using the heaven-herd as the conduit of his message when his people needed it. And Zulu practice had always acknowledged the power of the God of the Sky. Only an extreme situation, however, that went beyond the needs of individuals to that of the society as a whole could transform traditional roles. Zulu society, by the turn of the century, was in desperate straits. Their land had been taken away, their king exiled, their religion called into question by Christian missionaries. Their young men had been torn out of the fabric of village life and sent to the mines many hundreds of miles away. All these factors conspired to create a crisis in Zulu life and thought. Shembe's message showed a way out of this crisis for some. And so his message took hold. It pointed the way to a kind of healing available to those who felt the suffering most severely. The message had a new form, but it was familiar enough to be heard and understood.

But the relationship between Christianity and traditional Zulu religion worked in the opposite direction as well. Because the Zulu acknowledged the reality of the God of the Sky, their religious system provided a meeting point with Christianity. Christians could appeal to this meeting point as the bridge over which elements, at least, of their religious world could journey and gain entrance to the system of the Zulu people. But the character of the God of the Sky became in the process transformed from a remote creator and sustainer of the world who was appealed to only in time of dire need, or when the forces of nature threatened destruction, into a God closer at hand. Isaiah Shembe was one bridge for this encounter between two religious worlds. In one mind and in one movement we can see the Zulu religious world making an accommodation and creative response to a new situation while at the same time maintaining its own coherence and integrity. The Christian world tended to make exclusive claims, but the Zulu system as transformed in the mind and movement of Shembe tended to be inclusive; that is, it contained both Christian and Zulu elements.

Shembe's movement was not alone in its confrontation with the world of the whites. The oppression and suffering experienced by the Zulu was fertile ground for the emergence of other movements. One of these was the Ethiopian churches. These churches did not encourage the role of the prophetic and even revolutionary leader represented in Shembe's person and movement. Instead they emphasized the importance of organization and adaptability to the new situation in which the Zulu found themselves. Whereas Shembe's movement was radically anti-white in sentiment, the Ethiopian churches were ambivalent about the oppressors. They imitated white modes of organization in their churches, and the ministers of the churches were expected to be pastors, leaders of the flock.

Once again we need to be reminded that in the religious world of the Zulu the headman/priest is that official who assumes responsibility for the entire life of the kraal. We must add to this the importance given to rank throughout Zulu society. Now in a new setting that calls forth creative responses to new situations, it is this role of the headman/priest that becomes transformed into that of the church leader, who emphasizes diplomacy and rank. What is old is the emphasis upon the centrality of headman/priest; what is new is the Christian imagery that is added to the traditional system. Whereas Shembe's movement transformed the role of the heaven-herd, the Ethiopian churches transformed the role of the headman/priest. In both cases the traditional system has roles that are flexible enough to be interpreted in new ways when warranted. In both cases traditional values are maintained even as they become filled with partially new content.

In South Africa there have been two standard responses to white oppression by the Zulu, that of accommodation and that of resistance. These responses have assumed not only a political form but also a religious one. And very often these responses to oppression have been combined in one movement. Among the Zulu it is very difficult to finally separate the religious and the political. Though no Zulu chief accepts white oppression, the Zulu chief has tended to be more accommodating than leaders of the various movements for liberation that have developed in South Africa.

This standard form of accommodation had failed; new forms of action were required. The Ethiopian church created a new form of expression of the traditional role. There is still accommodation, but of an ambivalent kind. Their church "is as good as the church of the whites," because it has the same forms of organization, the same type of leadership. But their church is their own; it is a black church, a Zulu church with its own access to power. One might have to live under the numbing shadow of the whites, but one could still live according to the resources of one's own traditions.

What is most interesting is that many Zulu have insisted upon maintaining the traditional system without resorting to such new interpretations. For them the religious system they have inherited makes sense no matter what the world is like. These Zulu continue to regard the kraal and the hills as the locus of religious activity; the God of the Sky, the ancestors, medicine, and evil are the powers to be reckoned with. And the traditional roles designed to bring these powers to bear on their lives are still valued, for that is what it means to live one's life as a Zulu. From their point of view, their thought and practice has never been understood by the whites in any case. When the Christian missionaries, in all their sincerity, translated the Bible into Zulu, they called their Christian God Unkulunkulu, thinking that that was the name of the Zulu God. But for the Zulu, Unkulunkulu was the first man, not the God of the Sky. This first man was a creator, however. After having come from the sky he was the creative source of all other human beings. The Christians showed their inability to understand by confusing two different roles.

Nevertheless, even "traditionalists" have demonstrated a remarkable capacity for recognizing what is of value in the thoughts and actions of the people who came from across the sea. The values of a formal educational system, the discoveries of science, the political and social theories that describe and explain human behavior have all made an impression. And many Zulu have set as their goal the acquisition of new knowledge in whatever context it is available. Some of the white universities have been accessible, and some have not. When they are accessible, the Zulu have used them for their own purposes. When they are not, the Zulu have devised their own means for educating themselves. The Zulu have demonstrated that they are willing to face the challenges of a new world and have the resources to meet the challenge no matter what the whites have decided about the meaning and end of Zulu life.

What emerges is that the religious system of the Zulu continues in various creative ways to provide a foundation for the Zulu to live in a new world with dignity and grace. This world is a world *in* transformation and a world *of* transformations. We have been looking at a dynamic, not a static, tradition. As a tradition *in* the process of transformation, its world provides a context and a means for living in and thinking about the natural and social worlds. We have caught glimpses of what that world is like by becoming acquainted with its places, roles, powers, and actions, and we have learned something about such a world in action. We have also observed its ability to express itself in new ways; it has provided a bridge to other worlds, including that of Western medicine, and traffic over the bridge moves in both directions.

It is also a world *of* transformations. Transformation here does not refer to a process of change and accommodation but to the complex relationships that exist within the religious system. This means that within one system there are alternative modes of thought and action but one alternative receives its significance only in relationship to the other alternatives. For example, the position of men and women differ in the Zulu world. And yet these positions have a relationship to each other. Though the headman/priest provides the link between the present and the past, between the living and the dead, between the world of everyday life and the world of ancestral power, nevertheless women have an alternative access to the sources of power through divination, witchcraft, and special rites that are their exclusive province.

It is a world of transformation also because new religious forms are not simply alien, imported forms but responses to what is new and strange and attractive on the basis of a coherent system of thought and action. In Chapter IV we shall see just how such a system provides answers to important questions about what is real, important, personal, dangerous, and desirable. We shall also discover that the Zulu system, though it has some elements in common with Yoruba religion, also has a distinctiveness and integrity of its own.

CHAPTER III

The Yoruba and Their Religious Tradition

The Origins of the Yoruba People

The modern state of Nigeria is a large and complex country consisting of diverse ethnic groups with different languages, traditions, and religious systems. One of these groups of people is known as the Yoruba. They live in the western part of Nigeria and continue to practice their own traditions. Our purpose in this chapter is to describe their religion.

As with any culture in which the traditions of origins are preserved orally, the details of the beginnings of Yoruba culture are difficult to specify with any degree of accuracy. What is clear for the Yoruba is that there is a continuity to their culture that stretches into the very distant past. Many contemporary Yoruba have spent a great deal of time dealing with the question of their origins. Some have gone so far as to postulate a relationship with Middle Eastern countries. Linguistics and archaeology have been important tools in these investigations. We do know that a city such as **Ife** was founded nearly a thousand years ago and has continuously been a center of Yoruba religion ever since. Whether the establishment of the Yoruba people as a distinct tradition is traceable to migrations of people from the Middle East, or whether they are the result of a culture born of contact between indigenous African forest people and people from the dry regions beyond the Niger River is immaterial for our purpose, because we shall be examining the religious thought and practice of a people who now possess a very ancient heritage by now.

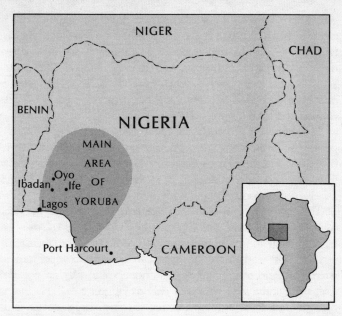

Yorubaland in the context of Nigeria.

Who are these Yoruba people, then? Estimates of their number vary according to the references one consults. There seem to be anywhere from five million to ten million Yoruba. The largest number live in the western part of Nigeria, but others can be found in Ghana, Togo, and Dahomey. During the period of slavery many of them were taken by force to the New World. Some people of African descent still practice at least some aspects of Yoruba tradition in Cuba, Brazil, and even the United States. There are residents of New York City who still perform rituals in honor of the Yoruba divinity Sango.

Though all Yoruba speak a common language and subscribe to the same world view, they actually consist of a number of social and political groups. Each of these groups, with its own tradition, has had a specific urban center. Each of these centers has an **oba** (chief) as the symbol of supreme authority, authority both political and religious in nature.

Each of these cities provides the focus for one of the various social groups in Yorubaland; nevertheless, the city of Ife was and still is regarded by the Yoruba as the center of their culture and religion. Each of the urban centers traces its own origin to Ife. New chiefs receive confirmation of their status from the paramount chief of Ife. Though other cities, such as Oyo, have, on occasion, had greater military and political strength, none has been able to supplant the cultural and religious pre-eminence of Ife.

The dominant occupation of the Yoruba is farming. Although people live in the cities, these cities are surrounded by farms where they work. On these farms secondary dwellings are built, especially if the farm is a long distance from the city, but these second houses are never as important as the primary dwelling in the city.

The Yoruba have had a much lighter contact with the forces of colonialism than the Zulu. Whereas the Zulu suffered colonization by the British and the expansion of the Afrikaaners into their territory and, further, became subservient to an imposed white state in which they and other indigenous Africans could play no political role, the Yoruba were subjected only to indirect rule. This meant that the traditional Yoruba structure remained largely intact. Nor did the British permit immigration of white colonists into the country. Hence the Yoruba never had to contend with a large alien population.

But external influences have had their effect on Yoruba culture. Both Islam and Christianity have developed roots within Yoruba society. Actually the influence of Islam preceded Christian missionary activity by a number of centuries. Some scholars date the introduction of Islam to the seventeenth century. Christianity was introduced in 1842 but was at first most successful with the newly freed slaves, who in turn attempted to spread it among the indigenous Yoruba. This meant the establishment of mission churches and, after some time, the development of independent African Christian churches.

In 1960 Nigeria, of which Yorubaland is an important part, was granted its independence and became a member of the British Commonwealth. Contemporary Nigeria is a complex mix of old and new. Skyscrapers, universities, and banks can be found in many of the cities. But along with these new symbols of contemporary life, the traditions of the Yoruba survive. It is to these traditions that we now turn our attention.

The Religious System of the Yoruba People

As with the Zulu people, the historical origins and development of Yoruba religion are too complex and too indefinite for a quick summary. Therefore, rather than discussing such problematic matters, we shall focus our attention upon the coherent world view of the Yoruba people. We shall proceed on the basis that there is both underlying unity and great diversity in the religious thought and practice of these people.

The diversity of Yoruba thought and practice is so great that some scholars—tongue in cheek—recommend studying its art instead. But there is little reason to be intimidated by the complexity, because Yoruba scholars have themselves already demonstrated elements of unity in the religious world view that underlies the thought and practice of the Yoruba. We shall use the results of such scholarship in our own description of Yoruba religion.[4]

Whereas the religious world of the Zulu is centered upon prac-

A specialist in healing performing a healing ritual. Photograph by Raymond Prince.

A Yoruba Egungun masked
dancer. Photograph by
William Bascom. Used
with permission of Lowie
Museum of Anthropology,
University of California,
Berkeley.

tices in the kraal and the hills, the Yoruba system has a dual focus.
On the one hand, it has its foundation in the city of Ife as the center
of all religious power. On the other hand, it is represented in every
compound, city, shrine, grove, temple, rock, tree, hill, crossroads,
diviner, priest, chief, family head in the land. Ife is the center because it was there that the god **Orisa-nla** commenced with the very
first acts of creation. But all the other places and roles are sources of
power also, because they derive their status from Ife.

In any religion there will not only be ritual action but people who
are responsible for ensuring that such action occurs. These ritual
practitioners either perform these actions themselves or direct those
who do. In this section I shall briefly identify the roles assumed by
the ritual practitioners.

In each Yoruba household, if the vitality of the religious symbols
is still treasured, there will be found a family shrine. It is at this
shrine that the head of the family, known as the **olori ebi**, assumes

ritual powers for communicating with the objects of devotion. Of particular importance is his ritual relationship with the ancestors, who are regarded as being important sources of power. No important event in the household can occur without the olori ebi's involvement. For example, the birth of a child, the departure of a daughter to be married, and the funeral of a family member will all require his guidance and his ritual action. Any infraction of the rules of Yoruba life on the part of a family member will be brought to his attention; it is his obligation to mete out the appropriate punishment and to perform the correct rites to the ancestors who have been offended by such infractions.

Whereas among the Zulu nearly all the ritual activity is concentrated in and around the kraal, among the Yoruba one finds different levels of ritual action. One level is the home, and it is the family head who provides the center of action. The second level is the town or city, and it is the town *oba* (chief, leader) who assumes ritual responsibility. The oba is the ruler or king or paramount chief of the Yoruba town. In the Yoruba view all such rulers originally came from Ife, for it was there that the gods established the earthly kingdom. In traditional Yoruba thought each oba is invested with religious power. In fact, their very position means that they are below only the gods in both power and status and, therefore, worthy of great respect. Without the presence of the oba certain rituals would not be performed. The oba, then, controls a level of religious power above that of the family head. There are annual festivals at which his presence is required.

At yet another level it is the oba and the priests of Ife who provide the focus of religious action. And intersecting all these levels are the priests associated with the many shrines in Yorubaland, who mediate between the human and the divine worlds. It should be clear, then, that we are dealing with a very complex system of ritual relationships and roles. One way of increasing our understanding of these roles, relationships, and objects of devotion is to identify the role of the priests in the religious system.

Among the Yoruba there are many gods, and each of these divine beings is attended by a priesthood. One kind of priest or **aworo** is the *babalawo*, or diviner. It is he who communicates with **Orunmila** (the god most closely associated with Ife) through divination and who is most frequently consulted by the Yoruba for advice about all matters of importance. Becoming a babalawo, or diviner, involves a long training period. But all the other priests also have an important function to perform in the religious system. They are in charge of the many shrines and are associated with one of the many divinities worshipped in the various areas of Yorubaland. Particular urban centers have particular divinities associated with them, and particular Yoruba will develop a ritual relationship to one or more of the shrines in the area. These priests are responsible for the sacrifices performed by the devotees of a particular divinity and communicate the commands and wishes of the gods to the people. They are also responsible for arranging the many festivals that are characteristic of Yorubaland.

In addition to the priestly role there is that of the medium or **elegun**, he or she who is spiritually possessed. Among the Zulu, divine possession (either by trance, dream, or sign) was a condition for being called to perform the role of the diviner, but among the Yoruba anyone can become a medium for divine powers without becoming a diviner. In fact, in the context of a religious festival such experiences of possession frequently occur. In such ecstatic states the divine powers communicate through the elegun, the one who has become possessed, to the other worshipers. But such an experience does not lead to the assumption of a ritual role like that of the Yoruba diviner, which takes many years of training and most probably involves having inherited the calling.

The role of the specialist in medicine is very similar to that in the Zulu system. Though all Yoruba have knowledge of medicine, the *oloogun,* the specialist in identifying the causes and prescribing the cures for the various illnesses that beset the Yoruba, plays a key role. He is the repository of medicinal knowledge. What is particularly interesting is that he usually works in cooperation with the babalawo, for it is he as diviner who is suppposed to be particularly adept at uncovering the reasons for an illness. But medicine is not an autonomous system. Its power comes from the gods. In that sense the oloogun is a conduit for healing power.

The **egungun** are masked dancers who perform at festivals and other important ritual occasions. They wear nets over their faces to prevent their identification, wear long and colorful robes, and are regarded as the representatives of the ancestors. The masks they wear are handed down from generation to generation and are seen by the Yoruba as possessing great power. Special rites must be performed by the men who wear them, and they are believed to be particularly dangerous to women. But there is one woman who is permitted contact with them; she is known as the iya agan, and it is her function to supervise the dressing of the egungun.

Each of these roles provides an access to one or more aspects of the world of power. The most inclusive symbol for that world is the Yoruba concept of Orun. In our discussion of religious powers in the following section we shall describe the many ways in which Orun is the locus for such power.

The Yoruba divide the cosmos into two parts, Orun and Aiye. Orun is heaven, or the sky, and is the abode of the High God, known by two names, Olorun and Olodumare. (For the purpose of this discussion, the High God will be referred to as Olorun.) It is also the abode of the other gods (known as orisa) and the ancestors. It is populated with other sources of religious power also. Aiye is the earth, the world of human habitation. In this second world live people and animals and "the children of the world," known as *omor-aiye*. This latter group is responsible for sorcery and witchcraft. It is clear, then, that both heaven and earth contain many sources of power.

Although Yoruba cosmology is complex and not centered in one deity or principle, it is possible to understand it by seeing it as organized according to three main elements located at three levels. Olorun is the chief source of power. He is also the most remote, and in the world of worship, he is never approached directly. The orisa represent a level of power that is approachable through ritual action and so provide one very important focus for Yoruba religion. The ancestors exist at yet another level of power. On the level of family worship, they assume an important place in religious activity.

All these sources of power have an intricate relationship to each other. We shall first describe some of their features and then attempt to clarify some of the relationships.

The Yoruba word *Olorun* literally means "owner of the sky" and refers to the High God who lives in the heavens. But there is a considerable range of opinion among the Yoruba themselves about his nature and origin. Some see it as an additional concept added to the indigenous religion under the influence of Christianity and Islam.

Other Yoruba think that it is a long-standing concept in the indigenous religion and integral to the Yoruba world view. From their point of view, the Yoruba were quite capable of conceiving of a High God apart from external religious influences.

Such diversity of opinion reflects a more general problem in Western scholarship about the nature and origin of the High God in the development of religion. Some Western scholars think that the High God occurs early in the emergence of religion. Others, using an evolutionary metaphor, argue for the late development of the concept and give particular credit to the Jewish, Christian, and Muslim religions for its discovery.

What version of these views one adopts, however, is irrelevant for our purposes, because it is generally agreed that Olorun has played a significant role in Yoruba religious thought for some time and that he does represent the most basic level of religious power.

Olorun is the originating power in the cosmos. All other powers, such as the orisa, the ancestors, and, in fact, all forms of life, owe their form and being to him. But he has delegated many of his powers to the other divinities. An elaborate system of mediators is interposed between him and the world of human life.

Thus Olorun is often regarded as austere, remote, and difficult to approach. Although he is prayed to, no shrines are erected in his honor, no rituals are directed toward him, and no sacrifices are made to placate him. Such religious activities are to be directed to the gods at a lower level of power. They are the ones who act as mediators between this world and the other world. And they were brought into being in order to serve the purposes of Olorun.

Some scholars refer to the orisa of Yoruba religion as lesser divinities or lesser deities. The fact is that these gods are regarded by the ritual practitioners as a source of religious power that can act for their good or ill, and they are an important focal point for religious action. The point in the religious system of the Yoruba is that there are many such foci, and their power is based finally on the power of the High God.

Who are these orisa? There are many of them. And their large number corresponds to the variety of forms that Yoruba religion takes. A particular orisa may only be worshiped by one descent group in one town. And there he or she will have a shrine for that purpose. Another orisa may be regional in influence and may, therefore, be worshiped at a number of shrines. Some orisa are worshiped throughout Yorubaland. All this is an indication of the diversity of religious expression in Yoruba religion.

The orisa provide a key focus for religious worship among the Yoruba. Some Yoruba claim that there are over four hundred of them. We shall pay attention to only a few; the ones we have chosen are widely known throughout Yorubaland.

Orisa-nla, also known as Obatala, is one of the orisa worshiped throughout Yorubaland. He has many religious functions, one of the most important being his role in the creation of the earth and the bringing to earth of the first sixteen persons already created by Olorun. Orisa-nla is, in fact, credited with the sculpting or shaping of the first humans and, interestingly, is also responsible for the existence of albinos, hunchbacks, cripples, dwarfs, and mutes. These unfortunate people are not regarded as having been punished but as being sacred; they are meant to remind the more fortunate of their obligation to worship Orisa-nla.

Two important taboos are associated with him, against drinking palm wine, and against having any contact with dogs. He has a particular association with the color white; he is said to live in a white palace and to wear white raiment, and his followers often wear white clothes. He is the chief of the "white gods," of whom there seem to be about fifty. But there is a problem here, because these may simply be different names for the same god. He has a priesthood associated with him, and shrines in his honor are to be found throughout the country where sacrifices to him are regularly made.

As has been mentioned, there is more than one version of the creation story among the Yoruba. In the tradition held at the city of Ife it is **Oduduwa** who pre-empts the role of creation normally associated with Orisa-nla. This story says that Orisa-nla became drunk with palm wine and failed to follow Olorun's instructions correctly, and Oduduwa therefore had to rectify Olorun's errors. Whereas Orisa-nla is clearly a male deity, the status of Oduduwa is not nearly as clear. In some versions "he" is the wife of Orisa-nla. Scholars argue that the various stories reflect layers of tradition, with Oduduwa replacing Orisa-nla in ritual importance. What is perhaps most interesting about Oduduwa is that he is also regarded as having at one time been human; at his death he was transformed into an ancestor with the status of an orisa.

Orisa-nla is worshiped throughout Yorubaland; Oduduwa has shrines and a priesthood mainly in the city of Ife. But because of his association with this sacred city, he is, nevertheless, recognized as an important deity throughout the land.

Orunmila is that god with whom the practice of **ifa**, a method for acquiring knowledge through divination, is associated. In fact, some also refer to him as Ifa, but Yoruba scholars regard this as a confusion between the practice of divination and the object of divination. In any case Orunmila is a god with great knowledge and wisdom, who was present at the creation of the human race and has knowledge of human destiny. It is particularly appropriate, therefore, that he be the source of information about the future of humankind.

An important element in the Yoruba religious system is that the destiny or fate of humankind was decided by Olorun from the very beginning, that humans have forgotten their fate, and that such knowledge can be recovered through the process of divination (ifa).

Esu is one of the most complex of the Yoruba deities. Christian missionaries, in their early encounters with Yoruba religion, tended to equate him with the concept of the Devil, but this is most unfortunate and distorts his nature, because, though he has certain evil properties, he is by no means the incarnation of evil. In Yoruba religion Esu is regarded as having taught Orunmila the secrets of divination. He is also an important extension of Olorun's power. In fact, it is one of his major roles to provide tests for the people in order to determine their character. He is also conceived of as a mediating power between heaven and earth; any sacrifice to the orisa must include a portion for him to ensure his cooperation in mediating between the two worlds. Failure to perform the appropriate obligations to the orisa brings about Esu's wrath and consequent punishment. Proper respect for the divine powers brings about his suitable rewards.

The complexity of Esu's nature is revealed by his tendency to incite the Yoruba ritual practitioner to give offense to the other orisa by failing to sacrifice to them. But this aspect of his character can also be misinterpreted, for his intention is to ensure that, as a consequence of such offense, the ritual practitioner will then perform the sacrifices required as a result of the offense. This ensures the continuing worship of the gods.

Although Esu is an important deity and is constantly on the minds of the worshipers, he has no special set of worshipers and no special shrine. Instead, all places of worship and all acts of worship contain a place for him. As a result he is an object of indirect attention even when other orisa are the focus of a ritual act.

It is precisely because Esu contains within himself forces both of good and evil, both reverence and irreverence, and encourages both worship and giving offense that he is able to mediate between heaven and earth. It is his contrary qualities that make it possible for him to assume the key role of mediator between the many levels of power conceived of in Yoruba thought, particularly between the worlds of divine and human power.

Esu, then, is the ambiguous god. **Trickster**, mischiefmaker, punisher, rewarder, source of wisdom and knowledge, confuser of situations, mediator—all of these things can be said of him. A failure to understand Esu's role in the Yoruba religious system is a failure to understand the lineaments of that world.

Esu may be one of the most complex of the Yoruba gods, but **Ogun** is one of the most puzzling. He is variously regarded as one of the original gods and as a human ancestor who became a god. The puzzlement might be removed by looking closely at his characteristics.

According to the religious traditions of the city of Ife, Ogun was its first king. It should be remembered that, according to Yoruba tradition, all kings originally were descendants of the first king of Ife, where the world was established by the gods and where the gods first expressed their power. Having been established at Ife as its first ruler, Ogun ruled the city and its territories as a chief is supposed to. His people were obliged to be obedient and respectful towards him. But some of his people failed to show proper respect. As a result of this insult, Ogun lost control of himself and started to kill his own subjects. When he realized the gravity of his acts, he killed himself with his own sword and disappeared into the bosom of the earth. His last words were a promise to respond to those who called upon him in dire need.

Now, according to Yoruba tradition, Ogun is the god of metals and war. There are also traditions that emphasize it was Ogun who, with his metal ax, cleared the path for the other divinities when they came to the earth. Thus Ogun has a special relation to all acts of tool making and all functions and roles associated with these acts. The Yoruba know that the discovery of metals and the making of tools was later than the act of creation and yet is a fundamental and creative step forward in human progress. Also, such implements are capable of both destructive and constructive use. As such they have both a divine and a human element, and thus both the divine and the human worlds are credited with this great discovery. Ogun's status reflects this duality. Ogun is associated both with the heavens and the earth. His abode is both in the heavens and on (or under) the earth. He is both a living god and a dead ancestor. If one were to place the gods on a line extending from Olorun to the ancestors, Ogun would be on the borderline between the gods and the ancestors. It is this special place that makes it possible for Ogun to stand for justice, the justice of the gods and the justice required in human action. In courts of law, Yoruba who still live by their traditional customs swear to tell the truth by kissing a piece of iron in the name of Ogun. And because of his association with metals, drivers of motor vehicles of all sorts often carry a representation of Ogun as a charm to prevent accidents and ensure their own safety.

We have already seen how important the ancestors were in Zulu religion; they are equally important in Yoruba religion. We have also seen that among the Zulu there is clear distinction between the God of the Sky (and the heavenly Princess) and the sacred ancestors. In Yoruba religion, not only is the world of the divine divided into the High God and the orisa, but the world of the ancestors is similarly divided. So whereas in the religious system of the Zulu there is a single source of power in the sky and a single source of power in the earth, in the Yoruba world there are dual sources of power in the sky and dual sources of power in the earth.

In the Yoruba religion the ancestors are religious powers capable of acting for the good or ill of their descendants. Therefore the ancestors are treated with great respect and devotion. In fact, special shrines and rituals exist as contexts for maintaining proper relationships with them.

There are two classes of ancestors, family ancestors and "deified" ancestors. We shall discuss these two classes of ancestors separately. As with the Zulu, not all people who have died become ancestors, or at least ancestors to whom any ritual attention is paid. Special qualities are required for there to be such ritual attention. The most important quality in a family ancestor is having lived a good life, and as a consequence, having achieved the state of *orun rere*, which literally means being in the "good heaven," the world of Olorun and the orisa. The next important quality is the attainment of a ripe old age, for this is a good indication that one has fulfilled one's destiny. Yet another quality is the possession of dutiful descendants who remember the ancestor with appreciation and are willing to continue to perform the ceremonies in his honor.

Such ancestors will be venerated or worshiped by their descendants and will be represented by the egungun; the Yoruba believe that the ancestors are ritually present in these masked dancers. Such ritual practitioners become conduits for messages from and to the ancestors and, in fact, assume the role of mediators between the family and the departed loved ones. On special occasions, for example at a festival, all the ancestors may be brought back and represented by many egungun. In many regions of Yorubaland such festivals are eagerly awaited and provide a focus for community celebrations; they may even be linked to the planting of the new crops for the year.

The "deified ancestors" are tied not to particular families but to the history of the cities or to important factors in the development of Yoruba culture. These ancestors have shrines not simply in the home but in towns, often throughout the country. Some scholars, in fact, refer to them as orisa. Whatever the term used, such ancestors are considerable sources of power, and in fact, ritual practices are associated with them. Sango, Orisa-oko, and Ayelala are examples of ancestors who have attained a very special status in Yoruba religion, although in some cases their influence does not spread throughout the country. Sango has a specific association with lightning, Orisa-oko with farming, and Ayelala with punishment for wrongdoing. What is interesting is that their human origins are preserved in Yoruba stories; what is not in doubt is their ability to exert power for good or ill and the necessity of worshiping them.

We now have a picture of the many places of religious action in Yoruba religion, the different roles assumed by the religious practitioners, and the levels of religious power addressed in the wide variety of rituals. But one additional concept is needed to understand how places, roles, and religious powers are related to each other, namely, the concept of mediation.

In the Yoruba religious system mediation plays a particularly important part. Mediation occurs in many contexts, involves many agents, and implicates many sources of power. The first of these contexts is that of the family. As we have already learned, the family head is the key ritual figure in this context, and one of his most important functions is to maintain ritual relationships with the ancestors. He is the channel for communication with the ancestors, and as such a channel, he acts as a mediating agent between heaven and earth—but with a specific focus upon the family ancestors. He represents the people to the ancestors by sacrificing to the ancestors on behalf of the people, and he represents the ancestors to the people by informing the family members of their obligations to the ancestors.

On special occasions, however, the ancestors are represented by the egungun (masked dancers) rather than by the family head. One such occasion is the death of an important family member. After such a death the egungun will emerge from the house of the deceased, imitate this newly departed person, and convey messages of consolation from him to the living members of the family.

The second context for mediation is that of the shrine. Here it is the priest of the particular form of Yoruba religion practiced in the area who assumes the mediating role between the member of the cult and the particular orisa. For example, if the orisa is Orunmila, the god of divination, then a babalawo (one of the many kinds of priests) will be the mediating link between the devotee and Orunmila, the keeper of his destiny.

The third context for mediation is that of the city. Here the mediator is the chief, who, by virtue of his direct descent from the original kings of the sacred city of Ife, is capable of representing the entire population of a city and its environs to the orisa. His mediating role is expressed in many ways. For example, on festival occasions he will be the leader of the procession, and his important role will signal the presence of the orisa. In fact, some festivals cannot proceed without his mediating presence.

The fourth context for mediation is every act of worship in which one orisa is required to mediate between the ritual practitioner and another orisa. The clearest example of this is the role of the orisa Esu, who, though possessing no shrines of his own, is always acknowledged whenever the worshiper sacrifices to another orisa. Failure to

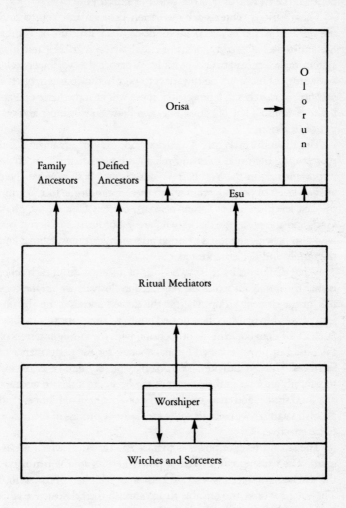

Figure 3

acknowledge the mediating role of Esu will abort communication between the worshiper and the world of sacred power.

These various contexts for mediation between the Yoruba and the world of sacred powers point to the complex structure of Yoruba life and reflect the many forms of ritual action that their religious system makes necessary and possible. Whether the worshiper seeks knowledge of his or her destiny, pays respect to the deceased, offers a sacrifice, or marches in a procession, there will be a mediator operating to establish a line of communication between worshiper and object of devotion.

The diagram in Figure 3 provides one way of organizing and representing the ritual roles and religious powers that play such an important part in the Yoruba religious system. It shows that there are two levels of power, within which there are multiple foci. Within the first level, known as Orun (heaven), there is Olorun, the High God, and the orisa, the deities who are subordinate to Olorun but who also provide the focus of ritual attention for the worshiper and the family and deified ancestors.

What distinguishes these two kinds of ancestors from each other is that the family ancestors are venerated exclusively within the context of the descent group whereas the deified ancestors are the objects of worship of a specific cult tied not to a family but to a locality. Such a cult does not exist in competition with the family ancestors or the orisa but provides an additional context for the performance of sacrifices. Thus an individual Yoruba may be found to be sacrificing to a family ancestor in the context of the home, to a deified ancestor at a local shrine, and to an orisa at a regional or national shrine. And all such sacrifices will require some mediator or process of mediation to be effective.

The second level of power is that of *Aye* (or Aiye) which means earth. The worshiper is a focus of power here as are the **omoraye**, the witches and sorcerers who are known as "children of the earth." These are *not* orisa and are able to accomplish their destructive aims by manipulating and twisting the human personality.

Having described the roles and powers, the process of mediation, and the various contexts in which the powers are addressed, we shall now illustrate how all these factors operate in specific situations. There is no better place to start such an analysis than with that most characteristic of all Yoruba religious practices, divination, or ifa.

A Babalawo performing Ifa divination.
Photograph by William R. Bascom. Used with the permission of the
Lowie Museum of Anthropology, University of California, Berkeley.

The Yoruba people practice many forms of divination. The most widespread and highly regarded of these is the consultation of the divine oracle. In observing a divination ritual one will notice that there are three elements in the ritual: the diviner, who is known as a babalawo, the ritual apparatus that the diviner uses in the consultation, and the person who is consulting with the diviner. In order to understand what is occurring, we need to know something about the Yoruba concept of the person, something about the diviner and the consulter, and something about the procedures and objects used in divination.

In Yoruba religion each person is regarded as both a physical and a spiritual being. The physical aspect of the person is known as *ara*. This is the word for the body of the person. The spiritual aspect is described in two ways, first as *emi*, or "breath," and second as *ori*, or "head." Without emi, which is that power that gives life to the body, there would be no person at all. Without ori the human body would be incapable of thought and be unable to communicate with the world of religious power. One of the most important aspects of ori is its relationship to the course of the life of the individual. Each person has chosen his or her identity before birth, and that identity includes a life plan that is that person's fate. Because this identity has a heavenly origin, it is also the guardian of that individual and is identified with an ancestor. Each person, therefore, can also be considered as the reincarnation of an ancestor.

Each person, because of his or her ori, is of spiritual origin, having come from the domain of the ancestors, the world of Orun. Birth into this world is accompanied by a failure of memory. Such a memory of destiny needs to be recovered or rediscovered. Consulting the divining oracle fulfills that function. Therefore, when consulting the oracle through the mediation of the diviner, a Yoruba is attempting to come to terms with his or her destiny. Although such destiny has the ring of inevitability about it, nevertheless, it needs to be "protected" by ritual action and discovered through the knowledge available through the diviner. It also is capable of being "modified" under certain conditions.

And so the Yoruba consults the diviner, the babalawo. Who is this ritual practitioner? The babalawo is one of many kinds of priests to be found in Yoruba religion, because each god has his or her own priesthood. The babalawo is the priest who has a special ritual relationship to the god Orunmila. *Babalawo* literally means "father of secret things." The babalawo is the priest who through the process of divination mediates between human and divine and reveals the human patterns of destiny.

The procedures and objects used in the divining process are as follows: When the Yoruba who desires to consult an oracle comes to the diviner, the diviner arranges the ritual elements and prepares for the act of divination. The elements are sixteen palm nuts (or a divining chain), a divining board, and divining powder. If the diviner uses the palm nut method (and this is regarded as more reliable than the chain) he will place the sixteen nuts in his left hand and then attempt to take as many of them with his right hand as possible. If only one nut remains, then he will make a double mark in the divining powder on the divining board. If two nuts remain, he will make a single mark. If no nuts or more than two remain, he will make no marks. The purpose is to end with two columns with four sets of marks in each column. A particular result might look as follows:

//   /

/   //

//   /

//   //

There are 256 possible combinations of such marks. Each of these sets of marks has a set of traditional stories associated with it. The babalawo will know at least four such parables, or Odu, for each of these 256 sets. Experienced babalawo will have memorized many more. In fact the diviner's expertise is measured by the amount of wisdom in the form of such parables that he knows. When a particular set has been arrived at by the diviner and the appropriate story has been chosen, he will inform the consulter what action the story recommends be performed. A sacrifice of some kind will almost always be part of the requirement, because sacrifice is the basic form of communication with the religious powers.

In this act of divination, then, one has a number of elements: a world view in which a forgotten destiny needs to be discovered, an action that must be performed to keep this destiny on course, a method for determining the action, a priest who is expert at determining the problem to be solved and the means for solving it, and a consulter with a problem. To understand the operation of these key elements is to understand something about the Yoruba view of how one's destiny can be both discovered and ensured.

Destiny is not, however, only an individual matter; it also involves the future course of community life and experience.

In a world in which farming is still the predominant activity, one of the most important annual events involving matters of destiny is the harvesting of crops. Nowhere is the delicate system of equilibrium that binds gods and people together more obvious and more immediate. A good crop means plenty, and a poor crop means famine.

One of the most important crops of the Yoruba is yams. They are a staple in the Yoruba diet, and much depends upon their bounty. Because orisa, ancestors, and humans are mutually interrelated, all are involved in the success or failure of the crops. The harvest festival provides a context for the establishment and maintenance of these relationships; the roles of the people and the sacred powers are particularly important for the destiny of the crops.

One such festival is the New Yam festival, known in some parts of Yorubaland as Eje.[5] In this annual festival the god of the sea, Malokun, plays an important role, but many other types and levels of religious power play a part as well. In fact, the entire range of religious power from the ancestors to the gods becomes involved in this celebration.

The festival lasts for two days and consists of a number of activities: purification rites, presentation rites, divining rites, and thanksgiving rites. On the first day it is important to ritually purify the areas in which the rites will take place. Two such places are the sacred grove and the sacred shrine. After these areas have been purified, the rest of the festival may proceed. The yams have already been taken to the oba's farm, where they have been placed in heaps. These yams must be presented in a ritual manner to the appropriate religious powers. Some of them are placed at the shrine of the orisa Malokun. Upon their arrival, which is announced in a loud voice, the people congregate together to joyously welcome the new harvest. A new year is about to be born, and the priest of the shrine prays it will be a good and successful one.

On the night of the first day of Eje, after the yams have been installed in the shrine, the people remain outside, where they give continual thanks to the religious powers generally and address the ancestors specifically, making offerings of palm wine and kola nuts to them.

But although the yams are already in the shrine, they have not yet been formally offered in sacrifice and have not played a role in divination. The ritual of presentation to the orisa involves a number of elements. First is the requirement that both oba and priests purify themselves by fasting throughout the day. On the morning of the second day the oba, dressed in a white garment, makes an offering of a white kola nut and a white pigeon and prays with the priests to Malokun. This is followed by a procession to the shrine, where the yams are now presented to the religious powers, namely, Malokun and the ancestors.

One of the high points of the festival is the divination rite that will determine the destiny of the life of the community, especially the success or failure of the crops in the following year. In this rite one of the recently harvested yams is taken and divided into two parts. They are cast, and if one falls face up and the other face down everybody is pleased, for this is a positive sign. If both fall either face downward or face upward there is concern, for it indicates problems ahead.

Another ceremony, also involving divination, then takes place in the other sacred area, the grove. The people all move in a procession to the grove, where, once again, a yam is divided and its two parts cast in an act of divination. And once again there is rejoicing if the signs are positive and concern if they are negative. The people and the priests then proceed to the palace, where they are met by the oba, who then joins the procession and leads them in a dance through the town. An important part of this dancing procession is the stops it makes at each of the shrines of the many divinities worshiped in the town. Sacrifices are made to the orisa venerated at each shrine. The fast of oba and priests is then broken, and a general celebration begins. The town has been purified, the yams have been presented; the future has been divined; the orisa and the ancestors have been served; and the new year has begun when new crops can be planted with confidence that the act of divination has ensured their destiny.

One way of understanding a religious system better is to see how it defines the important events in the life of an individual. We shall follow the career of an individual from birth to death and show how key elements of the religious system make their presence felt in the stages on life's way. The information we shall use is a summary of extended discussions the author has held with Yoruba informants. The individual whose career we shall be tracing will be called Ogunbode Akinsaya. Ogunbode is his religious name, and Akinsaya is his family name.

One of the first actions that Ogunbode's mother performed, when she discovered that she was pregnant, was to pay a call on the diviner (babalawo) who was resident in her city. There were two purposes for her visit: first, to have him divine the destiny of the unborn child and, second, to have him both prescribe the right medicines to take to ensure a good birth and tell her which taboos to observe. The medicines would be decided by a consultation between the diviner and a specialist in medicines.

Having performed these important tasks, she returned home and began her preparations for the birth of the child. Very soon after the child was born, he was taken to the babalawo, who again performed the divining ritual to determine the child's destiny. After knowledge of his destiny was acquired, the parents made an offering at the shrine of the orisa named Ogun, because it was to him that Ogunbode's family felt the deepest attachment and around whom a great deal of their religious life was centered. The offering that the parents made was a sacrifice and was regarded by them as being crucial for maintaining a correct relationship with him in a time of danger. They were also very careful to include a portion of the sacrifice for Esu to avoid any mischief from this powerful and puzzling orisa.

Because Ogunbode was a boy he was given his name on the ninth day of his birth. Had his mother given birth to a girl the naming ceremony would have taken place on the seventh day. If twins had been born they would have been named on the eighth day. His name, Ogunbode, was chosen by his parents because of their religious relationship to Ogun and was one of a set of possible names that exist to honor this orisa. The other names in the set are Ogunlake, Ogundolam, Ogunyale, Ogunsanya, and Ogundele. A name, then, gives to its bearer an obvious and immediate connection to the divine world.

From the time of Ogunbode's birth certain foods were automatically forbidden to him. His parents knew what food to withhold because of what the diviner had already said. But such a set of taboos was not permanent, for in the process of growing up he could decide to eat what was forbidden when he observed someone else doing so. But the decision was Ogunbode's own.

Ogunbode's place of residence was not with his mother and father but with his grandfather, who, because of his status as family head (*olori ebi*), was the most direct link with the family ancestors. Ogunbode was from the very beginning of his life taught both the ritual and the family responsibilities that go with being a Yoruba who still believes in the importance of the ancestral traditions. As well as learning the religious traditions, Ogunbode also learned from his grandfather the intricacies of farm work, for the compound in the city had its own farm in the countryside.

Before he reached his second birthday Ogunbode was circumcised. No special ceremonies of a religious nature, that is, having any reference to either the ancestors or the orisa, were performed at this time. This act was simply to ensure that he would have an important qualification for marriage, because no Yoruba male can be married without having undergone circumcision.

From his earliest days Ogunbode was regarded as being part of an age group. This meant that boys of roughly the same age formed a community of their own. The same was true for the girls. All through his life his friends and acquaintances would have a special attachment to him because of his relationship to such an age group.

More than one informant has told the author that there are only three important events in the career of a person, namely birth, marriage, and death. Aside, therefore, from the act of circumcision and Ogunbode's participation in the life and experiences of all those belonging to his age group, nothing of religious significance characterized his development until he was ready for marriage.

When he was ready for marriage, Ogunbode faced two alternatives. Either he could have an arranged marriage (perhaps his parents had already made a commitment a long time ago to some other family) or he could have informed his parents that a particular young woman had caught his eye and he wished them to start inquiries and negotiations about her availability. In Ogunbode's own case, he fell in love with an attractive young woman in his own city and so wished his parents to make it possible for them to be married.

It was at this point that mediation between the two families became important. Not only is mediation a fundamental process in Yoruba religion; it is also fundamental in Yoruba life. In a ritual context it involves the establishment of relationships by a ritual official between the human and the divine worlds. In matters such as marriage it involves the establishment of connections between family groups by the intervention of a middle person.

Such a middle person, or mediator, is known as the alarena, and it is her role to ensure that the proper procedures are followed in the intricate negotiations that take place. The particular functions of the alarena in this case were to know or to learn about the family of Ogunbode's prospective bride. Such negotiations always take a great deal of time, and the attitude of the bride-to-be's parents is crucial for a successful completion to the maneuvers. But finally the future bride's parents were sufficiently convinced of the good character of Ogunbode, and the parents of Ogunbode about the qualities of the future bride, to proceed with the arrangements. At this stage the future bride's parents arranged a consultation with the diviner, in the presence of the alarena, in order to determine the prospects for the marriage that both families knew had already been determined by the orisa.

In this particular case the diviner predicted a good and fruitful marriage for the young couple. Secure in this information, but also to ensure that this destiny came to pass, Ogunbode then went to Ogun's shrine and offered there a sacrifice to him and Esu.

All the right actions having been performed, Ogunbode was now ready to talk, for the first time, to his future bride. And his parents, secure in their knowledge that the marriage was destined to be a good one, arranged the bride price, once again through the intermediary. The wedding date was then set. This date could either be seven, fourteen, or twenty-one days after the completion of the final arrangements.

On the day of the wedding two sets of ceremonies, independent of each other, took place in each of the two family compounds. At the bride's house, aside from the expected festivities of eating and dancing, the women in the compound performed a ritual in which they circled the compound both weeping and chanting *okun iyawa*, which are special sayings such as "I am leaving for my husband's house; pray for me that I will have children."

At the compound of the bridegroom there was general revelry and much eating, drinking, and dancing along with an air of expectancy and excitement as they awaited the appearance of the bride. In both compounds sacrifices were performed by the family head to ensure the blessings of the ancestors on the marriage.

As the time came for the bride to leave she made a special visit to the family head in her own compound. All her attendants accompanied her on this visit, and when they arrived in his presence they respectfully seated themselves around him and silently listened to him pray to the ancestors in her behalf.

In the meantime the women from the bridegroom's compound had come to the bride's compound but had not entered through its gates. Instead they waited outside and could be heard continually chanting, "We are ready to take our wife." Upon hearing this persistent chanting, the bride knew that the time had come to leave. She covered her head and was led out by her own attendants. They introduced her to her new escorts, who then proceeded with her to her new home.

At the entrance of her new home a calabash had been placed in a conspicuous position. She was expected to shatter the calabash with a strong blow. The number of pieces into which the calabash broke was an indication of the number of children she would bear.

Then she entered the compound. There near the entrance her legs were washed, and she was taken to the oldest woman living in the compound. This old woman then led her to the family head of the compound, and she was introduced to him as the most junior wife of the compound. After the introduction to the family head, she was then introduced to the other family members living in the compound. Conspicuous by his absence during these introductions was Ogunbode himself, who was not permitted to be in the compound during these ceremonies. It was more important that his bride become part of the family and recognize where the family and ritual authority lay. In fact Ogunbode was not permitted to have any contact with his new bride on this first day. Only on the following day, perhaps even the third day, was he finally permitted to see her and then, on the evening of that day, to consummate their marriage.

Ogunbode lived to a ripe old age. When his father died, he became the new family head in his compound, and when he died all the many members of his family were notified of the event. Unlike the death of a child or a young person, there was no particular urgency to bury him. Thus there was time for all the relatives to gather together from far and near.

Ogunbode had done a great deal of hunting in his lifetime and, therefore, much firing of guns into the air took place. Some of the male members of the family even went on a brief hunting expedition into the forest to try to kill an elephant in his memory.

Very soon after his death his body was thoroughly washed and then laid out in his hut. He was dressed in the finest clothes, and a bed was made out of the best wood available. His grave was dug in the compound. If he had been a Christian he would have had the option of being buried in the local cemetery. But even Christians do not particularly care for such a practice. According to Yoruba tradition, burial in the compound, the home of the ancestors as well as the living, is the most desirable. Because Ogunbode was a follower of Ogun, the Christian alternative would not even have been considered.

The grave was dug with the help of the other followers of Ogun. But because Ogunbode died in old age, the babalawo was not consulted about the cause of his death. Only when someone dies young would the bereaved members of the family seek to identify the causes of such an untimely event. But the priests from Ogun's shrine were in attendance, and after his body was placed on the specially made bed that had already been placed in the grave, they prayed that he would be accepted into the good heaven (orun rere) and be judged worthy of taking his place with the ancestors. The priests also made a sacrifice to Ogun. Then the egungun masked dancers emerged from Ogunbode's hut and danced throughout the compound. There was further feasting and dancing, and all the visiting relatives slowly took their leave.

At the burial spot a new shrine was erected, for here a new ancestor would now be called upon and praises sung to his name. Ogunbode the ancestor would continue to be present in this compound and make his presence felt in many ways.

Transformations of the Religious System

No religious system remains static over time; new conditions and new discoveries change it in significant ways. Perhaps one of the most serious challenges to any system is contact with new religious systems. All religions experience it, and Yoruba religion, like Zulu religion, is no exception. Long before the coming of Islam and Christianity, Yoruba religion was in a constant process of transformation. In fact the term *Yoruba* itself seems to be a rather recent (nineteenth century) innovation in describing a large group of people with important connections to each other.

Islam and Christianity brought with them novel religious systems, which the Yoruba responded to in a number of ways. Some adopted the new religions; others attempted to maintain their traditions; still others developed new religious forms that transformed the newly introduced religious ideas into the terms of the traditional system. These complex responses brought even greater diversity to the religious life of the Yoruba. We shall attempt to deal with one kind of response by discussing the **Aladura** religious movement, which will help us understand how new religious movements are not merely reactions to alien symbolic systems but creative responses to them. Such creativity transforms an old idea into a new one while maintaining much of the previous religious structure.

Although Christianity was reasonably successful in establishing itself in Yorubaland via the mission churches, both the external control of religious development and the form of religious worship clearly did not satisfy all those people who did develop an association with Christianity. The Aladura churches in particular show evidence of such dissatisfaction. Originally this movement was not intended to be an alternative to Christianity but a supplement to the Christian rituals and organization.[6]

There are two kinds of Aladura churches, the apostolic and the visionary. The apostolic churches in their organization and activities reflect many of the values and attitudes of the mission churches. The visionary churches are much freer in form. There has been considerable argument about whether these new religious movements are Christian or not. Certainly the mission churches regarded them with some hostility, seeing them as heretical offshoots. Whether these churches are to be regarded as Christian, however, is beside the point for our purposes: the practices of these churches are interesting for the information they provide about the creativity and flexibility of the traditional Yoruba religious system. Whether or not Christianity can claim them, they have a clear Yoruba quality.

We shall focus our attention on one of the Aladura religious movements, that of the Seraphim and Cherubim. In 1925 a young woman, fifteen years of age and named **Abiodun** Akinsowon, had a religious experience while watching the Corpus Christi procession in Lagos. According to her own account, one of the angels under the canopy that carried the Christian sacraments followed her home. There she became possessed and had visions of the heavens, received revelations, and successfully passed tests given to her in the state of possession. A man named Moses Orimolade was sent to pray for her. Abiodun then came out of the state of possession and shortly thereafter founded a society with the help of Orimolade. The society's name was given in a vision, **Egbe Serafu**, that is, the Seraphim Society, and all subsequent additions to the society's thought and practice were given by visions. The society began to flourish and attracted many people by its focus upon the importance of prayer and healing. The society also attacked the traditional Yoruba use of medicine and specific Yoruba gods. There were injunctions against possession of clay representations of the gods and all the many ritual uses of medicine to be found throughout Yorubaland. The movement achieved high visibility by organizing large processions each year to celebrate the original revelation. Though Abiodun was the

receiver of the revelation, Orimolade became the leader of the
movement and Abiodun his assistant. Her official title was Captain
Abiodun.

At a certain point a split developed in the movement between
Orimolade and Abiodun. This first split was by no means the last
one, and various forms of Seraphim became established in various
cities. The movement continues to be strong to the present day, despite its fracture into a number of movements.

From its beginning the movement has emphasized the importance of prayer. The name Aladura means "the ones who pray," and
the movement believes that God always answers the prayers of his
followers. The movement has also stressed the importance of dreams
and visions, which are viewed as the sources of information and direction. They illuminate the causes of problems and identify courses
of action to be taken. As such, they become the means by which the
members of the movement can focus their prayers, and a special
time is set aside for the recording and reporting of these dreams and
visions. We have already made it clear that the Seraphim Society
was not intended to replace the Christian churches but to supplement them by stressing the importance of prayer in daily life. Much
of its imagery is Christian, but with novel twists. For example, the
following hymn is sung:

Witches cannot control us
Under the war-staff of Jesus;
Before the Seraphim,
All witches jump out of the way;
Holy Michael
Is the Captain of our society.

Many of the themes of the Seraphim Society are apparent in these
verses, and it would be easy to interpret the movement as a form of
Christianity. But such an interpretation would not account for the
success of the movement among the Yoruba. Whatever success the
movement has had depends on the traditional forms available for
transformation in the light of special conditions and upon the characteristics of the people who become involved in the movement. In
fact, many members were already involved in other Christian
churches and became attracted to Aladura.

One of the attractions of the movement lies in its reordering of traditional symbols. For example, the existence and power of witches is not denied, but the Archangel Michael can make them jump out of the way. The efficacy of traditional medicines is not denied. It is superseded by the power of Christ. One of the many reasons that Yoruba Christians were attracted by Aladura was the emphasis upon the healing power of Christ and the opportunities this provided for a new form of "medicine." Though traditional medicine was attacked, the traditional emphasis upon the availability of healing power in a ritual context was not forgotten. Aladura transformed the form of healing, but not its importance, and made the means available for healing.

The Aladura do not practice divination in the traditional manner, but their emphasis upon the importance of dreams and visions reflects a continuing interest in the issues of destiny present in the traditional system. Thus the convert to Aladura is every bit as interested as the tradition-oriented Yoruba in knowing the future and what acts are to be performed in assuring progress in the right direction. God still decides human fate. Just as there is flexibility in the traditional Yoruba view—though one's fate has been decided, nevertheless adjustments are possible through sacrifice—so this same flexibility is revealed through the means of prayer and visions. God answers all prayers, and prayer changes things.

Processions are frequent in Yoruba life—in the Eje festival, for example, a key element was the procession led by the oba—so it should not surprise us that a procession provided a context for the revelation that Abiodun received. Processions are also an important element in many annual festivals. Pilgrimages to sacred groves and sacred hills are widespread annual events; the Aladura churches have transformed these in their own way to express their new religious forms. Nor should we be surprised that it was an angel who provided the medium for Abiodun's revelation; the angel was a physical representation of a source of power, and such representations are fundamental forms of Yoruba religious expression. The angel represents the element of mediation. The prominence of the Archangel Michael can be seen as a transformation of one of the Yoruba mediators. Michael and the other archangels have a religious connection with earth, air, fire, and water and are regarded as guarding the gates of heaven. They assume the same mediating function as some of the orisa do in the traditional Yoruba system. All of this demonstrates the flexibility of the religious system of the Yoruba and its internal power to make new forms out of old forms in the presence of new conditions. Therein lies the power of a religious system in concept and practice—in established and novel ways—to provide an intricate and interesting context for the living of a good life.

■

CHAPTER IV

Individuals, Roles, and Systems

Any religious tradition, seriously considered, presents a puzzle to the student. One of the most intriguing elements in this puzzle is the sheer variety of practices and beliefs one discovers as one begins to pay close attention to the religious tradition under investigation. This diversity is as characteristic of the religions of America as it is of the religions of other times and other places. Readers only have to examine the yellow pages of the telephone directory in their own community to recognize the diversity of names religions have. Of course, from the point of view of the participants of a specific religion, such diversity is relatively minor and trivial. What counts is the underlying unity. But the student of religion cannot afford to ignore such diversity. It must be dealt with.

One way of doing so is to imagine what religion in America looks like to a serious student from another culture. If, for example, a visitor from Yorubaland were to come to America to study Christianity, he or she would experience both familiarity and strangeness. Familiarity would stem from encounters with, and knowledge of, Christianity in Nigeria. We have already learned that Christianity has taken root in Nigeria and that it has assumed not only "standard" but also new forms. The strangeness the visitor would experience would come from the bewildering variety of forms that Christianity takes in America, forms that are not duplicated in Nigeria. This variety would be expressed in many ways: imposing cathedrals, suburban ranch-roofed churches, and storefronts with exotic-sounding names all compete for attention. Were the student to commence study of any one of these Christian churches, he or she would discover an even more interesting fact. Even within the limits of one church would be found great variations in practice and belief among the members of the congregation. It would not be at all surprising to hear the Yoruba student exclaim at a certain point: With all this diversity, what is American Christianity really like?

In the same way, an American student studying Yoruba religion in its own context would be struck by the variety of forms that it takes, both within one area and between various areas. Moving from Lagos to Oyo to Ife would disclose a wide range of practices, beliefs, and institutions. Further complicating the picture are many hybrid forms in which Christianity and Islam seem to have become united with the traditional forms of Yoruba religion. The wider the net is cast the more complex the picture becomes. At a certain point such a student might very well exclaim: Not only do I not know what Yoruba religion is, but I cannot even identify Christianity in this context.

Given such a complex picture, one could easily conclude that the religious tradition is chaos. Were one to do so, then understanding that religious tradition would be impossible: one can experience chaos, but one cannot understand it. Chaos means that there are no significant connections among the variations that one has discovered.

But neither the Western religions with which the reader is probably most familiar nor the African religions to which he or she has been introduced are nearly as chaotic as they appear. The constantly changing, kaleidoscopic image that appears through the viewfinder of our investigations can be analyzed to reveal the principles underlying the variations.

How we analyze this set of variations depends upon what we focus our attention on. There are three useful ways to bring order out of the apparent chaos. Each of them will permit us to make the problem of assembling the puzzle into a reasonably clear picture more manageable. The first way is to analyze the thought and practice of the individual participants in the religious tradition. We have already done some of this by examining the life stages of Bhudaza and Ogunbode. This is the most concrete level of analysis and permits us to get a view of religion as it appears to participants in it. It is also the level at which extreme variations will be discovered.

The second way is to analyze the religious roles available to, and occupied by, the individuals within a religious tradition. The emphasis here will be upon roles and not individuals. It became clear in our chapters on the Zulu and the Yoruba that, even when one does analyze the religious career of an individual, some reference to the roles characteristic of the religion is inevitable. For example, one can talk about the roles of the headman/priest, the diviner, and the herbalist in Zulu religion without any reference to the individuals that occupy those roles.

The third way is to attempt to discover the system of thought that underlies both the practices and the beliefs of individuals and the religious roles and their relationships to each other. Each of these topics, individuals, roles, and systems, will be discussed separately in the following sections.

Individuals

The diversity of a religious tradition becomes most apparent when one talks to its various participants. It seems that no two individuals do exactly the same things, think the same thoughts, or interpret the meaning and significance of what they do and think in the same way. This produces a context fraught with fascination and frustration. Obviously, the variety of beliefs and practices is interesting and can lead to all kinds of questions about such a wide range of human behavior. Equally obviously, it is frustrating when one wants to be able to identify in some relatively simple way what it is that one is studying.

Scholars have employed a number of methods to handle these variations. One is to search for representative informants, with the hope that some individuals might be found who have given serious thought to the unity underlying the diversity. In fact some scholars appear to have become quite adept at identifying particular people in a religious tradition who have developed a remarkable perceptiveness about the unity underlying the diversity in their tradition. Some of the most interesting work on African religions has been done by scholars who have lived with the Yoruba and the Zulu for long enough to be able to identify such individuals and record their own interpretations and accounts of their religious traditions.

But there are also problems with such an approach. How does one decide who is representative and who is not? For example, scholars studying the Yoruba have spent a great deal of time speaking to the diviners, and the diviners have not been at all hesitant to tell what Yoruba religion really is. But there are different diviners, not all of whom agree with each other. How does one know who is right? Further, even if the problem of representativeness could be solved, we are still left with the interpretations proposed by these apparent representatives; are the interpretations solutions to the problem of diversity or do they just add to it? Clearly the student of religion cannot ignore what the informant says, for what he or she says is itself an instance of religious reflection that must be accounted for. Such interpretations suggested by the informants must be analyzed; they are part of the puzzle. What is most significant about these interpretations is that they disclose that people within a religious tradition, even when they disagree with each other, do think that there is an underlying unity—even when they cannot articulate it.

Another approach to diversity has been statistical. Given a range of responses to a set of questions one can attempt to identify the frequency with which similar types of answers appear. Some scholars have used the questionnaire method to identify the common practices and beliefs of a wide range of people. This approach is something like taking the pulse of a large group of people at the same time; one can come up with averages. One of the advantages of such an approach is that if it is done over a sufficiently long period of time it will provide a picture not only of continuity but also change over time.

But this approach also brings problems. What questions are to appear on the questionnaire? To ask a question means that one will be making one or more assumptions. For example, if the question is about the relationship between political and religious institutions, the question might assume a radical discontinuity between these forms of human behavior.

But whether the student of African religions relies on representative informants, or statistical methods, or some other approach in order to deal with the diversity within a religious tradition, he or she will discover one very important fact, namely, that different individuals participate in a religion to different degrees and in different ways. In other words, there will be levels of participation in a religion and there will be different kinds of participation in that religious tradition. Some individuals will, according to their own lights, faithfully practice all or nearly all of the rites and duties made available to them in their own context. Others will practice only some of these rites and duties. And there will be a wide range between these extremes. It will be important to identify some of the reasons for varying degrees of participation.

Not all of the reasons will have to do with interest or commitment. For example, a Zulu working in the Johannesburg gold mines will not perform all of the rituals that he would were he still living in the kraal in Zululand. And we already know why from our study of the locus of religious action. In Zulu religion the primary places for ritual activity are in the kraal and on the sacred hills. The kraal is the abode of the ancestors, and it is there that they must be approached; they cannot be approached hundreds of miles away in a mining compound in Johannesburg. On the other hand, this Zulu mineworker might very well be found practicing rituals of sorcery and witchcraft. In fact, being removed from the environment of the ancestors automatically exposes him to the power of sorcerers and witches, and the best way to fight sorcery under such conditions of dislocation is with sorcery. So an examination of the context of the religious life of this particular Zulu will disclose that his actions differ both in range and in kind. In fact the amaNazaretha church in Johannesburg might provide him with a context for his religious life that both assures him of some continuity between his past and his present and (because of its differences with traditional Zulu religion) makes sense in such a strange situation.

In the case of the Yoruba a similar distinction between kind and degree of participation can be made. For example, a bank clerk working in the Nigerian city of Lagos, who was born and brought up in the city of Oyo, may occasionally make offerings at one or more of the many Yoruba shrines in the city. He may occasionally also consult a diviner. But his primary religious identification may still be with the particular traditions of his former city. In spite of this sense of identification he might also spend some of his religious energies in a Baptist church in Lagos. Yet whenever he returns to Oyo he might not only make offerings to his ancestors in the family compound but, if the season is right, participate in one of the annual festivals for Ogun. Thus to the student of African religions he might identify himself as a Christian of Baptist persuasion and yet be married in the traditional Yoruba manner characteristic of Oyo, and expect to be buried not in the Christian cemetery but in the family compound according to Yoruba custom. His degree of participation in Yoruba religion will differ from the family head who has remained in Oyo, and the kind of participation will differ also, because he is attempting to live both in a Christian religious world and a Yoruba one.

But individuals come and go, and Zulu and Yoruba religion remain. It is at this juncture that we need to recognize that there is more to a religion than the practices and beliefs of individuals. What this more is becomes clearer as we begin to examine the roles characteristically present in a religion.

Roles

Whereas a religious individual participates in a religious tradition according to circumstance, custom, and interest, the various roles characteristic of the religious system in which he or she participates are not nearly as flexible. There are usually "standard" roles in the religion that are defined by the system and not by the individuals who have a relationship to it. And there should be nothing surprising about this. The fact that there is a headman/priest, a diviner, a heaven-herd, and a herbalist in Zulu religion is not decided by a particular Zulu. It was there before they were born, and unless the religion completely disintegrates in their lifetime, it will be there after they have died. Of course, if the particular Zulu happens to be Isaiah Shembe and has a revelation and a call to establish a new form of worship, then what he does might very well have an impact on the total religious system. Under the impact of an Isaiah Shembe, the total system might change in some way or it might assume a number of different forms that continue on together. It is clear that some of the variation in a religious tradition can be accounted for by new experiences and new revelations that permit the establishment of new or transformed systems of thought and action. What all of this shows, then, is that, apart from the participation of individuals, and because of new revelations and new interpretations, a religious system has a history, which is to say that it can and does change. Both Zulu and Yoruba religion have been a long time in the making, and the many roles they contain are there by a complex evolution.

As we have indicated, it is possible for such a system, despite its long history, to collapse, and it will do so if it does not make sense to a sufficient number of individuals. No system can continue if the roles defined by the religious system are not occupied by individuals. But given a living religion with a history, we can examine the roles themselves and learn something about that religion without having to inspect what goes on in the mental life of the participants.

When we begin to examine the roles in Zulu and Yoruba religion one of the first discoveries we make is that no role in either religion makes sense in isolation. For example, to attempt to understand the role of the heaven-herd in the religious system of the Zulu without reference to the other seven roles leaves us with a picture of a disturbed individual standing in splendid isolation on a mountaintop speaking to bad weather. But when we examine the eight roles in their relationship to each other, we know that, in the context of the religious system of the Zulu, the heaven-herd and the headman/priest have opposite roles. The heaven-herd has a ritual relationship with the God of the Sky, whereas the headman/priest is the ritual mediator between the ancestors and the people of the kraal. But we also know that neither of these ritual functions is exclusively identified with the heaven-herd or the headman/priest. The supplicant also has access to the God of the Sky, and the diviner also can communicate with the ancestors on behalf of the people. In fact, once we know what the sources of power in Zulu religion are we can show that for each source of power there is a dual set of roles available in the system to make a connection between the human and the other world.

The more we learn about the relationships among the roles the more we can discover about the complex system of thought that is expressed not only in what the Zulu and the Yoruba say but in what they do, and what they take as important. In fact, examining the roles in their complex relationships leads us to the recognition that there is a structure to a religious tradition and that such a structure has a history. However we analyze this structure, we will discover that questions about one element will lead to questions about other elements. For example, questions about the role of the herbalist will

lead to questions about the ritual relationships between the specialists in medicine and the patients. They will also lead to questions
about the status of medicine as a power and to questions about the
destructive use of medicine in sorcery and witchcraft. And questions
about sorcery and witchcraft will lead to questions about the nature
and power of evil, the relationship between the power of the God of
the Sky, medicine, and evil, and the relationship of all these to the
power of the ancestors. They will also make possible questions
about Zulu views of the causes of evil and the role that diviners play
in disclosing good and evil.

In the structure of Yoruba religion a similar chain of questioning,
based upon our identification of Yoruba ritual roles, can be under-
taken. Because the roles vary from situation to situation, and because not all roles identified in Chapter III are found in every vari-
ant, we can analyze the roles according to one or more of their
functions. For example, mediation is a characteristic of Yoruba religion. Many of the roles provide the context and conduit for specific
relationships that individual Yoruba are attempting to establish between themselves and the sources of power. Examining the mediating function of a particular role will give us information not only
about the experience of the individual Yoruba worshiper but also
about the way that the role of the worshiper becomes connected via
the mediation of the babalawo to the role of Olorun, Esu, and a
particular sorcerer.

Let us examine, for example, the case of a worshiper who is faced
with a major decision about her occupation. She has decided to
move from the city of Oyo to Lagos to teach in a school. This worshiper has focused her religious energies on the god Ogun. She has
regularly sacrificed to him (and to Esu); she has regularly participat-
ed in his festivals. How does the role of such a worshiper make a
connection with the world of the gods? By paying a visit to the diviner or babalawo. The diviner represents the mediating role between the worshiper and her destiny. We already know that her destiny has been determined in the other world. So the diviner, on the
basis of manipulating the kola nuts, will provide her with the
knowledge of how to decide about the move. But the diviner will
also recommend that she make an offering to Ogun and Esu, for
only Ogun gives the power to act. But even this power to act can be
interfered with by Esu, so an offering must be made to him as well.

This offering will be made at a local shrine to Ogun, and at that shrine there will be a priest who is a mediator between the worshiper and Ogun. Thus the role of the diviner becomes linked with the role of the priest. But we also know that it is Orunmila, not Ogun, who is responsible for human destiny and divination that provides access to it. And so in the other world Ogun mediates between Orunmila and the priest who is mediating between the worshiper and Ogun. But what is most interesting of all is that, from a Yoruba point of view, the role of Ogun and Orunmila depends upon the role of the worshiper. The orisha depend upon the offerings for their power. They would be diminished without the sacrifices.

Another example of how the roles work and what they tell us about the structure of Yoruba religion, and the system of thought that such a structure represents, is that of a man beset by a serious illness. Upon consultation with the babalawo, the worshiper might discover that sorcery is involved. Now, in Yoruba religion sorcerers are human, not divine, powers; they are children of the world. They are able to accomplish what they do by virtue of the destructive resources within the human personality and not by a relationship to the orisa. They do not have to harness special evil powers or forces; they simply have to be adept at mischief and destruction. Now the worshiper in such a situation has a number of options available to him: He might attempt to counter sorcery with sorcery. Or he might try to deal with the threat by taking medicine from the oloogun, the specialist in medicine. Or he might attempt to call upon the power of the orisa. He might even call upon the power of the Aladura church, which is known for its power over sorcerers and witches. But whatever he does, he will consult the babalawo, for it is this kind of priest who has access to knowledge about the causes of the illness.

What we discover, then, is that there are a variety of roles relevant to this situation, that these roles have a connection with each other, and that the sources of power made available by the ritual roles can be in either heaven or earth. Not only is understanding the roles in all these examples impossible without seeing how they all fit together, but the practice of one role in one situation inevitably leads to the practice of another. So in either Zululand or Yorubaland, if you come across a diviner performing rituals, you will sooner or later discover that other roles have come into play as well.

But even a thorough knowledge of all the roles in all their contexts will not be adequate for understanding these two religions. We shall still have only partial knowledge of what these religions are. The reason has already become apparent: We could not discuss the roles in either Zulu or Yoruba religion apart from their reference to the sources of power that make them important to the individuals who occupy them. Individuals and roles are elements in a system that gives them their coherence and unity—the roles, and the experiences of individuals in all their variety, are expressions of a coherent system of thought. To discover what this system of thought is like is crucial, therefore, for understanding how the roles obtain their definition and the individuals their experience.

Systems

How, then, do we understand and describe such a system? Many analogies have been available, but one of the most useful is that of a language. A language has variants, a structure, and a dynamics. The variants of a language are known as dialects; these can be regional, occupational, or a matter of status or social level. In fact, one way of defining a language is as the sum of its variants. The structure of a language can be described in a number of ways. At its most basic level of analysis, a language consists of a set of sounds combined to form words. These words are combined to form sentences, and the sentences are combined to form either oral or written discourse. The dynamics of a language can be described by paying attention to the many uses to which it is put by its speakers. Most generally the dyamics disclose that language is a vehicle for both thought and action.

Like a language, a religious system has variants, as we have already seen in our discussion of the beliefs and practices of individuals. Such variants can also be regional, or a matter of religious roles or degree and level of participation. A religion, like a language, can also be defined as the sum of its variants. Where and when one analyzes it makes a difference to what one discovers. But just because there are variants does not mean that these variants are unrelated to each other. Just as the various English dialects are still English, so the variants of Yoruba and Zulu religion are still Yoruba and Zulu. In fact, one way of looking at these many variants is to understand them as transformations of each other, that is, different arrangements of certain elements that they have in common. One way of describing these elements is as a world view; this world view can be expressed in many different ways, in many variants. Different expressions bring into focus different arrangements of the elements. For example, in the Yoruba world view, there are Olorun, the orisa, the ancestors, and humans and all other forms of life. Each of these is a source of power, and ideally, each exists in a relationship of equilibrium with the others. But in a particular place, at a particular time, for particular reasons, only one of the orisa or one of the ancestors may be the focus of ritual action. And it is quite possible that, at least for a time, an entire tradition might develop around one source of power almost to the exclusion of all the others. Nevertheless, there will still be subtle ways in which the other sources of power are recognized and acknowledged.

We must, however, look beyond these variants in order to discover other interesting properties of the religions of Africa. We must also examine their structure and dynamics.

A structural analysis of a religious system, such as that of the Yoruba, will disclose that a religion, like a language, consists of a set of elements. These elements are the individual acts that occur in the course of religious behavior in general and ritual behavior in particular. A ritual consists of a set of acts. When we observe a sequence of these acts, we are, in fact, observing a ritual in progress. For example, if one is studying the marriage rites, one can show how individual acts form a sequence of acts and how a number of sequences form a very complex ceremony. One can concentrate on an analysis of the individual acts and talk about their meaning and importance, or one can concentrate upon a particular sequence of acts and show how they accomplish a specific objective—for example, how they change a man and a woman from the status of being unmarried to the status of being married, or how being married is part of an even larger picture that describes an entire style of life.

Paying attention to the dynamics of a religious system will clarify further of its characteristics, especially when we keep the language analogy in mind. Consider the many uses to which the sentences in a language can be put. We can ask questions and give answers. We can prohibit actions, command attention, tell the truth, conceal our motives, invent elaborate metaphors, speak in riddles, describe events, and imagine possible and impossible worlds. We can communicate or deliberately misinform, express our emotions, explain our theories, and state our beliefs. We can even play with words. In fact, the power of a language lies in its flexibility.

A religious system is equally flexible. Just as it is a mistake to think of a language as having only one purpose, so it is a mistake to think of religion as having a single purpose. Its infinitely large set of purposes is discovered according to the categories that one brings to the analysis. And it can be analyzed in its own terms or in terms originating outside of it. Consider, for example, Zulu religion in the context of a system of oppression. Such a religion in one of its variants can be analyzed in its own terms. So that when the Zulu speaks about "amandla" (power) as being necessary to overthrow the oppressors, such an appeal can be interpreted in Zulu terms as being a call to the ancestors, or the God of the Sky, or the power of medicine, to act in a certain way. But it is also possible to analyze this call to overthrow the oppressors in political terms that are "outside" the Zulu system of thought. Whichever way we proceed in such a case we must be careful not to conclude that the Zulu religious system is nothing but a political system, for it means more than that to them and it is more than that in any adequate theory.

The more deeply one analyzes a particular religious system, the more one tries to take into account the experiences and behavior of individuals, the complex and intricate relationships among the roles, the kinds and levels of power believed to be real, the more one discovers its importance for shaping human life for good or ill. And one can understand how its flexible forms can be used for the expression of compelling narratives, for solace and comfort in time of need, for an environment for reflection and meditation, as a rallying cry to overthrow the oppressors, or even as a divisive influence tearing family and even whole societies apart. It can become a vehicle for the expression of lofty and abstract thoughts, or an occasion for the cruel, the mean, and the petty.

Perhaps the most compelling analogy between a language and a religion is that a religion, like a language, provides a vehicle or a context for thought. In the case of a religion, it is not only what people say within the context of a particular ritual or series of rituals, or what they say about a particular ritual or series of rituals, that shows that we are dealing with a system of thought. The language of the particular people we are studying is itself the direct vehicle for the expression of their thoughts. What should be recognized is that systems of acts, and the relationships among the roles, are also vehicles for the expression of such thought. Ritual actions, roles, and relationships are, in fact, like statements, a special language expressing a form of knowledge. If one understands something about the system under study, one can show *how* it is, in fact, a system of knowledge.

One can learn about what the Yoruba and the Zulu take to be knowledge not only by talking to them but by seeing what they do, how they organize their lives, how they divide their time, what places they venerate, what kinds of relationships they value, what they welcome, and what they avoid. Chapters II and III have provided us with some of the information we need to engage in this task of analysis.

In what follows we shall attempt to show that on the basis of the information that we do have we can show how these two religious systems can be understood as systems of thought that provide answers to some quite specific questions.

Let us start with the Yoruba. If we grant that there is something called the Yoruba religious system and that it is contained not only in Yoruba words but also in Yoruba rituals, roles, and relationships, then in what sense does the Yoruba religious system deal with the question, what is real? The answer is both simple and complex. On the simple level it is that whatever has power is real. This answer is revealed not only in what the Yoruba say but in what they do. Their deeds as well as their words show what they regard as having power. On the most fundamental level Olorun, the High God, has power. His power has been illustrated by the creation of the world and the establishment of the city of Ife. The Yoruba, no matter what the change in political structure, no matter where the center of earthly authority lies, treat the city of Ife as the place where the High God has revealed his power and his intentions. Now, in virtue of the fact that Olorun has power, other forms have power, or are sources of power. So the orisa have power, as do the ancestors, chiefs and kings, family heads, priest, and, in fact, all human beings. In addition, other forms of life have power as well. Even inanimate objects, under certain ritual conditions, are sources of power. Medicine is particularly powerful for both good and ill. Even witches and sorcerers are sources of power. But there is an important difference between their power and all the other kinds. All the other kinds of power are part of a closely interrelated network. The major characteristic of this network is that unless it is disrupted it exists in a state of balance or equilibrium. Sorcerers and witches are perverted human beings; something has gone wrong with them or inside of them. As a consequence, they can upset the balance among the powers, with disastrous results for one or more members of the Yoruba community.

The second question to which the system provides an answer is, what is important? The answer is that it is important for human beings to discover their destiny and live according to it. Once again, this answer is not simply a verbal one that one might elicit from Yoruba who still attempt to be faithful to their tradition but one that can be discovered by observing what they do, what roles they take seriously, and what relationships they value. One discovers one's destiny by consulting a diviner and making one's decision in the context of what the kola nuts show and what the verses the diviner contains in his memory demonstrate. The act of divination presupposes that one's destiny has been decided in heaven. Such a destiny is both personal and social. On the personal level, it is the course of one's life. On the social level, it is the group fulfilling its obligations to all sources of power in heaven and on earth. This means respect for elders, deference to authority, and valuing traditional places, times, roles, and arrangements.

The third question is, What is a person? A person is a living being with a destiny determined in heaven. A person can either be balanced or unbalanced. A balanced person is one who "feeds his head," who makes the appropriate offerings to orisa and ancestors at their shrines and recognizes their presence within his or her own being. These sources of power are both far away and as close as one's own breath. They are both outside and inside. To the extent that they are within, one is oneself a source of power with the ability to make a difference to the world.

A balanced person is also one who honors ancestors. This means ensuring that they are buried in the right place and in the appropriate way. It also means continuing to revere them by making offerings to them, by consulting them about important decisions, and by not offending their memory.

A balanced person is one who performs the rituals to the orisa

and does not forget Esu. Which orisa one worships is a matter of
history, of geography, and of personal choice. In fact, the diversity in
Yoruba religion can be traced partly to this principle, namely, that
one's location in space determines the range of ritual choices and
ritual objects to which one can become related.

Finally, a balanced person is one who uses his or her own power
to maintain the orisa by participating in the rites and festivals, making offerings to the orisa and the ancestors, and preserving the traditions of the society. Without such human use of power, the gods
begin to lose their power and disappear from the scene.

An unbalanced person is an omoraiye, a "child of the earth."
This means a number of things. It means, first of all, the perversion
of human power for destructive ends. It is humans turning on humans to harm and destroy them. It means one who has been cut off
from heaven and lives only off the turmoil created by being out of
balance. It means acting in the terms of witchcraft and sorcery.

The discussion of an unbalanced person leads naturally, then, to
the next question to which the religious system of the Yoruba provides an answer: what is dangerous? Anything that upsets the intricate balances among the many sources of power in heaven and earth
is dangerous. Literally this means giving offense to any source of
power, whether this be another human, an ancestor, or an orisa. And
how does one give offense? By failing to recognize what is real, do
what is important (and not do what is forbidden), and live the way
a person in balance should live. A strong sense of tradition will show
the way, and divination will provide the details.

And what is the form for maintaining right relationships with all
sources of power? mediation. Mediating persons, roles, and objects
provide the forms for maintaining such relationships, whether it is
the alarena mediating a wedding contract, the priest mediating a
ritual offering, a babalawo mediating a decision concerning destiny,
or a set of kola nuts mediating an offense, in each case there is an
appropriate form available for the Yoruba person who wishes to remain in balance with that vast and intricate network that establishes
the structure of the world in which he or she lives.

It can be shown that the same questions are answered by the
Zulu system of religion. As we proceed, we shall also be able to note
certain similarities between the Zulu and the Yoruba forms of
thought, as well as important differences. What we cannot fail to

notice is that, if the analysis presented here is correct, then there is no basis for regarding these two societies as being primitive or irrational or bizarre.

To the question, What is real? the Zulu answer at the first level is remarkably similar to the Yoruba. Whatever has power (amandla) is real. But when we move up a level and analyze what is meant by the term *power*, that is, what the term applies to, then we note both important similarities and important differences between the two systems of thought. What has power in the Zulu system is the God of the Sky, the ancestors, and medicine. Sorcerers and witches have a derived power, but, whereas in Yoruba religion such beings are perverted human beings, in Zulu religion they are perversions of the total system of powers. Furthermore, whereas in the Yoruba system the orisa play an important and separate role from both the God on High and the ancestors, in the Zulu system no such separate source of power is available. This is not to say that there is no complexity in the God of the Sky. As we have already indicated in the chapter on the Zulu religious system, the heavenly Princess adds a dimension to the character of the source of power that the God of the Sky represents. But when we examine the actual rituals the Zulu perform, we see that only a certain set of women has ritual access to such a source of power.

The Zulu system also represents an answer to the question, What is important? Whereas the Yoruba system implies that it is important for a human being to discover his or her destiny and live according to it, the Zulu system implies that it is important for a human being to uncover the seeds of destruction that if permitted to grow will distort the orderly arrangements of social life. The method for the discovery of destructive elements and the maintenance of order can be either divination or the ordeal. Which of these it is depends upon the status, position, and nature of the people involved. For example, in the grouping-up ceremony it is the ordeal that overcomes the destructive elements and establishes order, but in the funeral ceremony it is divination that uncovers the cause of illness and death and medicine and traditional ritual that restore order. Personal destiny has nothing to do with it. As a consequence of this emphasis upon order, individualism is less possible in Zulu society than in Yoruba. Among the Yoruba there is always that element of choice, tied, of course, to the fact that each person does have a destiny decided in heaven.

What is a person? A person is a social being with intricate relationships and obligations to the members of the kraal and to the ancestors who dwell there. A person is also one who acknowledges that all the kraals are intricately related to each other by custom, ceremony, marriage, and tradition. There are some ancestors who not only have a primary identification with a particular kraal but an identification with all the Zulu people. These ancestors are acknowledged in the praise songs that all Zulu know. Although it is the obligation of a particular clan to remember, chant, and preserve these songs about the great cultural heroes, they are the heroes of all.

Thus, though the concept of balance and equilibrium is present, the possibility of that balance being disrupted is always real; the emphasis is not on balance but on praising the ancestors in song and maintaining right relationships with them.

What is dangerous? Whatever gives offense to the ancestors. To give offense to the ancestors, by not "bringing them home," by not acknowledging them in the appropriate rites in the umsamo, by arranging marriages without taking into account the ruptures caused by new alliances, all are examples of giving offense. This is doubly dangerous because, not only can the ancestors punish the offender, but by giving offense the offender rends the fabric of social life and opens the world to perversion of the sources of power exemplified in the activity of sorcerers and witches. In such a situation even the ancestors may be rendered ineffective.

What is the form for maintaining right relationships with the system of powers? The answer to this question depends upon the two contexts for ritual acts. As we have seen in Chapter II, these are the hills and the kraal. The hills are a natural, and the kraal a social, environment for religious action. Both provide places for communion with sacred power. In the natural environment the heaven-herd and the supplicant approach the God of the Sky directly and without mediation. So when the God of the Sky is the source of power with which right relationships must be established, the form is one of solitariness and isolation, away from the human, social world in the hills of God.

But when the ancestors are the source of power, the form is one of group activity mediated in every case by the precisely defined roles of the religious system. There is little question that this second context is in the foreground of Zulu religion. This is why the Zulu, although they acknowledge the importance of the God of the Sky in the creation of the natural world and the making of the first human, do not spend much time emphasizing this. The social world and the solidarity required of it are at the center of the stage. There are historical reasons for this view that lie deep in Zulu experience. These reasons go all the way back to Shaka's emphasis upon uniting many clans into one Zulu kingdom. Throughout their history there were persistent attempts from within the Zulu kingdom to destroy such solidarity. And their encounter with the territorial designs of the colonial powers demonstrated its importance again.

To this very day, the Zulu continue to emphasize such solidarity and to express it in their relationships both with the white people of South Africa and with the neighboring African groups with traditions of their own.

Tradition and Transformation

The answers to these sets of questions provided by these two systems of thought show that any claim that all African religions are alike is a very superficial one. On the contrary, they show different understandings of what the world is like and the place and power that humans have in it. There are obviously similarities—for example, both include the ancestors as an important source of power, and both take sorcery and witchcraft very seriously—but the systems differ greatly in the way they fit together. We are obviously dealing with two different religions with different elements and different views about how life is to be lived and reflected upon.

In the contemporary situation both Zulu and Yoruba face a complex future. Not only do both peoples have continuing and complex relationships with the other indigenous people around them, but they also have continuing and complex relationships with the worlds of Christianity and Islam. In addition, secular modes of thought and action that propose new concepts of power and new relationships to place and role continue to make their presence felt. It seems clear that Zulu and Yoruba systems of thought and action are flexible enough to respond to these different systems in a creative and responsible manner. Our discussion of traditions in transformation and transformations in tradition have attempted to provide a form for analyzing this process and set of relationships.

There is a re-emphasis upon the importance of their traditions among the many peoples of Nigeria today. In this context the Yoruba people are no exception. At the same time, in Nigeria generally and among the Yoruba in particular there is an emphasis upon new styles of decision making, new ways of advancing knowledge, new ways of developing relationships with the peoples of Africa and the rest of the world. It is as if there is a double movement. As a relief from the strictures of colonialism there is a re-emphasis upon Yoruba identity and the traditions that have defined it. The Yoruba have demonstrated a new pride in their cultural and religious heritage. At the same time new forms of thought, action, and organization continue to be taken seriously. We can expect this double movement of reappropriation and new appropriation to continue. World views are always in the making. But whatever the form and content of this new world view, we can reasonably expect that the Yoruba religious system will play a formative role in that process of transformation.

Among the Zulu there is also an acknowledgement of the importance of tradition. But whereas the Yoruba have experienced liberation from colonialism, none of the black people of South Africa, including the Zulu, have had this experience; they continue to live under the system of apartheid. In a situation of large-scale white oppression symbolized by the system of apartheid there is an increasing tendency to modify the emphasis upon Zulu identity with an increasing emphasis upon the unity of all the oppressed peoples of South Africa. Nevertheless, this emerging consensus of unity will draw on a set of symbols and images to apply to a revolutionary situation. One of these symbols has already achieved prominence in the resistance movement. The Zulu word for "power" is *amandla*, and it has become a symbol that signals not only that the Zulu have sources for resistance but that all the oppressed people of South Africa have similar resources. Accommodation is giving way to resistance, both passive and active. And other African peoples on the rest of the continent are beginning to support such resistance with action and not mere words. Whatever new worlds of thought and action emerge in both the Yoruba and the Zulu societies, they will have a continuity with the great traditions that characterize these two religions of Africa and illustrate the process of traditions in transformation and transformations in tradition.

Glossary

Abantu. Zulu word for "the people." This name occurs in all of the Bantu languages and has the same meaning in all of them.

Abathakati. The Zulu name for a witch, that special person who manipulates powers for evil and destructive ends.

Abiodun (Captain). The young woman who had a revelation that became the foundation for the Aladura Movement.

Afrikaaner. One of the two groups of white South Africans. This group traces its ancestry to the early Dutch settlers.

Aladura. A new religious movement among the Yoruba having connections to both traditional and Christian religious forms: literally, "those who pray."

Amalozi, amakhosi, amathonga, idlozi. Zulu words referring to the ancestors or ancestral spirits.

Amandla. The Zulu term for "power."

Apartheid. The doctrine of the white South African government that people of different races or colors should be kept separate from each other.

Assegai. Zulu term for the traditional Zulu spear.

Aworo. Yoruba term for priest.

Bantu. Zulu term for person; also occurs in other Bantu languages.

Boer. Another name for Afrikaaner, emphasizing the traditional occupation of farming.

Divination. A process of identifying the cause of a personal or social problem and the means for solving it or predicting its outcome, often using special techniques such as throwing bones or manipulating kola nuts.

Diviner. One who is qualified to engage in the art of divination.

Egbe Serafu. The Seraphim Society, based upon the revelation to Captain Abiodun.

Egungun. A Yoruba masked dancer.

Elegun. A person who is a medium and therefore capable of being possessed by a spiritual power.

Esu. A Yoruba God with both good and evil qualities. All Yoruba believe it important to sacrifice to him.

Ethiopian church. A form of Christianity with special African roots, especially in Ethiopia, that has spread to other parts of Africa including South Africa.

God of the Sky. The supreme deity of the Zulu people.

Heaven-herd (Izinyanga Zezulu). That ritual official in Zulu religion who is responsible for controlling the weather.

Herbalist. A medical specialist with knowledge of what will cure and what will harm people.

Idlozi. One of the Zulu words for ancestor or ancestral spirits. It also refers to an old person.

Ifa. A special form of Yoruba divination.

Ife. The most sacred city of Yorubaland, the place where the world began.

Ihlambo. The washing of spears.

Imbuzi yamakhubalo. "The goat of medicine."

Inkosi Yaphezulu. The Zulu God of the Sky.

Inkosi Yezulu. Another Zulu name for the God of the Sky.

Isibongo. Praise songs or praise poems of the Zulu which celebrate cultural heroes and important ancestors.

Izinyanga Zemithi. A Zulu specialist in medicines.

Izinyanga Zezulu (Heaven-herd). See Heaven-herd.

Izinyanga Zokwelapha. A Zulu specialist in healing.

Johannesburg. The largest city in South Africa and the center of the gold mining industry.

Kehla. Headring worn by Zulu as a signal that he is shortly to be married.

Luthuli, Albert. A famous Zulu chief who received the Nobel Peace Prize.

Medicine. A power in the Zulu religious system capable of good or ill and to which a ritual relationship is necessary.

Oba. The Yoruba term for a chief.

Odu. Parables used in Yoruba divination.

Oduduwa. A Yoruba god associated with the creation of the world and having a special connection to the city of Ife.

Ogun. The Yoruba god of iron.

Olori Ebi. The Yoruba term for head of the family.

Omoraye (Omoraiye). Earthly powers of destruction in Yoruba religion who engage in witchcraft and sorcery.

Orisa-nla. One of the Yoruba Gods worshiped throughout Yorubaland, regarded as having an important role in the creation of the world, particularly the sculpting of human beings.

Orunmila. The god most closely associated with the practice of Ifa.

Oyo. An important city in Yorubaland and the center of political power in important periods of Yoruba history.

Qhumbaza. Zulu term for ear-piercing.

Shaka. The Zulu chief who welded many diverse clans into one powerful Zulu nation.

Shembe, Isaiah. A Zulu prophet who established the amaNazaretha Church in South Africa.

Sorcery. An activity similar to, but not as destructive as, witchcraft in which people and/or events are manipulated by special means.

Thomba. Puberty rite among the Zulu.

Trickster. A spiritual or superhuman being with a capacity for good or evil and a tendency to trick people to their discomfort, detriment, and occasionally, salvation.

Ukubuthwa. The growing-up ritual.

Ukubuyisa idlozi. The ritual performed by the Zulu to "bring home the ancestor." Often abbreviated to Ukubuyisa.

Umfaan. A young Zulu boy who is responsible for herding the cattle.

Umnumzane. The head of the Zulu kraal.

Umsamo. The special place in the Umnumzane's hut in the Zulu kraal where the ancestors are communicated with and worshiped.

Witchcraft. The use of special techniques by a witch to destroy accepted social structures and to cause death to individuals.

Yoruba. An individual member of a group of people with a long historical and cultural tradition traceable at least to the founding of the city of Ife.

Zionist. A member of one of the Zionist churches in South Africa in which the symbol of "Zion" plays an important role.

Zulu. A member of the former Zulu kingdom with a historical and cultural tradition traceable to Chief Zulu, at present a "tribal group" in South Africa.

Notes

1. See Axel-Ivar Berglund's *Zulu Thought Patterns and Symbolism*. London: C. Hurst, 1976, p. 35 for a discussion of the use of praise names for Umvelingqangi.

2. For a detailed analysis of funeral practices see Eileen Jensen Krige. *The Social System of the Zulus*. 2nd Edition. Pietermaritzburg: 1949, p. 159–175.

3. The best complete description of the stages on life's way can be found in Krige, op. cit. p. 81–119.

4. Especially J. S. Eades' *The Yoruba Today*. Cambridge: Cambridge University Press, 1980, and J. Omosade Awolalu's *Yoruba Beliefs and Sacrificial Rites*. London: Longman, 1979.

5. For a firsthand description of the Eje festival see Awolalu, op. cit. p. 144–147.

6. The most thorough and systematic treatment of this movement remains J. D. Y. Peel's *Aladura: A Religious Movement Among the Yoruba*. Oxford: Oxord University Press, 1968.

Selected Reading List

Awolalu, J. Omosade. *Yoruba Beliefs and Sacrificial Rites.* London: Longman, 1979.

Berglund, Axel-Ivar. *Zulu Thought-Patterns and Symbolism.* London: C. Hurst, 1976.

Biobaku, S. O., ed. *Sources of Yoruba History.* Oxford: Clarendon Press, 1973.

Bryant, A. T. *The Zulu People as They Were Before the White Man Came.* Pietermaritzburg: 1949.

Callan, Edward. *Albert John Luthuli and the South African Race Conflict.* Kalamazoo: Western Michigan University, 1962.

Calloway, Rev. Canon. *The Religious System of the Amazulu.* London: Turner, 1870.

————. *Nursery Tales, Traditions and Histories.* Westport: Negro Universities Press, 1970.

Cope, Trevor, ed. *Izibongo: Zulu Praise-Poems.* Collected by James Stuart, translated by Daniel Malcolm. Oxford: Clarendon Press, 1968.

Cowley, Cecil. *Kwa Zulu: Queen Mkabi's Story.* Cape Town: C. Struik, 1966.

Dennett, R. E. *Nigerian Studies or The Religious and Political System of the Yoruba.* London: Frank Cass, 1968.

Eades, J. S. *The Yoruba Today.* Cambridge: Cambridge University Press, 1980.

Gleason, Judith. *Orisha: The Gods of Yorubaland.* New York: Atheneum, 1973.

Gonzalez-Wippler, Migene. *Santeria: African Magic in Latin America.* New York: The Julian Press, 1973.

Guy, Jeff. *The Destruction of the Zulu Kingdom.* London: Longman, 1979.

Hastings, Adrian. *A History of African Christianity, 1950–1975.* Cambridge: Cambridge University Press, 1979.

Idowu, E. Bolaji. *Olodumare: God in Yoruba Belief.* New York: Frederick A. Praeger, 1963.

Krapf-Askari, Eva. *Yoruba Towns and Cities.* Oxford: Clarendon Press, 1969.

Krige, Eileen Jensen. *The Social System of the Zulus.* 2nd ed. Pietermaritzburg: Shuter & Shooter, 1950.

Lucas, J. Olumide. *The Religion of the Yorubas.* Lagos: C. M. S. Bookshop, 1948.

Niven, C. R. *A Short History of the Yoruba Peoples.* London: Longmans, Green, 1958.

Oduyaye, Modupe. *The Vocabulary of Yoruba Religious Discourse.* Ibadan: Daystar Press, 1971.

Peel, J. D. Y. *Aladura: A Religious Movement Among the Yoruba.* Oxford: Oxford University Press, 1968.

Soyinka, Wole. *Ake: The Years of Childhood.* New York: Vintage Books, 1981.

Sundkler, Bengt G. M. *Bantu Prophets in South Africa.* 2nd ed. Oxford: Oxford University Press, 1961.